" There are few who have been at the cutting edge of the consumer megachurch movement, and the missional microchurch movement and are still doing the work with relevance and insight. In fact, I can only think of one—Ralph Moore. I have considered Ralph as my mentor for 30 years now, and I am still gaining new insights and helpful encouragement from him. This book is exactly what is needed for this moment. The only secret I wish I could extract from him now is how to remain young, vital, and ahead of the curve for so long."

Neil Cole
Author and catalyst of global organic church movements

" Ralph Moore is equal parts in-the-trenches leader and experienced mentor. He seeks to walk with his readers through the enormous cultural shifts the Church is facing today and to provide new, yet ancient, answers to the questions that burn inside those who long to see lives transformed by Jesus. God has worked in unique ways in each chapter of the Church's history, and Ralph shows us that the future of God's mission looks less like inviting people into programs led by professionals, and more like equipping all of Jesus' followers to bring the gospel to the world. Many church leaders struggle to escape the gravitational pull of what has worked before but is no longer working, myself included. Ralph has encouraged, challenged, and guided me to take the steps of faith that I already knew God was calling me to, and I believe this book will do the same for all who read it."

Pete Dahlem
Lead Pastor, Harvest Mission Community Church

" Over the decades, there has been no one better than Ralph Moore in navigating the Church through currents of change while revitalizing staid mindsets. Here he does it yet again in a timely and prophetic fashion. With clarity and simplicity, he tandems can-do thinking with can-do equipping for every believer. Read, and get ready to reproduce. This book will cause the gospel to go viral and holds real keys to revival—a work for such a time as this."

Norman Nakanishi
Founder and Executive Expansion Pastor, Pearlside Church

" Ralph Moore has done it again. He is a culture de-coder. Over 20 years ago I read my first Moore book, in which he insightfully taught on the uniqueness of Generation X and what it would take to reach them. Now he helps make sense of the current, confusing, cultural climate we—the Church—find ourselves in. Yet again, he prophetically and practically challenges us to leave the dwindling, safe enclave of last generation's Christianity to bravely venture outside the comforts of the four walls of the church to reach a tumultuous lost world. Get ready to have your thinking challenged and your heart inspired!"

Robert Herber
Pastor, All Peoples Church San Diego
Senior Leader, All Peoples Global

" Ralph Moore knows what he's talking about! I know that personally. Over the past two and a half years, through the COVID pandemic, Ralph has coached the pastoral leadership team of our church using the principles found in his most recent book, *Equipping Everyday Missionaries in a Post-Christian Era*. As a result, our once megachurch—built on a seeker model of programs and *adding* members—is effectively transitioning to a multiplication model of 'disciples making disciples who make disciples.' Thank God! In Ralph's own words, 'It's time for another awakening!' I couldn't agree more. May the Lord use the timeless principles in this book to inspire an awakening in our own time. In all of our churches. For His glory!"

Kip Jacob
Lead Pastor, SouthLake Church, Portland, Oregon

" Are you looking for a fresh take on leading new outreach-oriented churches into an optimistic future? In *Equipping Everyday Missionaries in a Post-Christian Era*, Ralph Moore guides church leaders through the essential paradigm shifts necessary for leadership in our post-Christian culture. Moore doesn't hold back from sharing his insightful personal experiences of leading multiplication movements, and his bent to provide practical tips and tactics is extremely helpful. This book will inspire, challenge, and help you start disciple-making movements that will undoubtedly lead to exponential fruitfulness in the Kingdom of God."

Dr. Ed Love
Executive Director of Church Multiplication and Discipleship
for The Wesleyan Church

" *Equipping Everyday Missionaries in a Post-Christian Era* is a valuable resource for pastors, leaders, and anyone who desires to make disciples. Ralph Moore not only leverages his five decades of ministry experience, wisdom, and prophetic insights into this book but creates a handbook for leaders to implement immediately within any context. Ralph shares practical tools to equip everyday missionaries to live out the mission of the Church. He also addresses the changes that must take place to create a disciple-making movement inside the Church while not overlooking the cultural challenges likely to be experienced beyond it. *Equipping Everyday Missionaries* not only identifies the limitations of the current operating system that most churches have implemented, but offers a much-needed practical, useful, and effective upgrade. This book delivers and compels all of us to live out the mission and lead others into it."

Antoine Lassiter
Lead Pastor, Think Kingdom Church, Charlotte, North Carolina
Church planter and church planting strategist

" I still remember reading *Let Go of the Ring* by Ralph. In it, he challenged us to consider the Hope Chapel story and its implications on us as church leaders.

In this book, the challenge is to change the way that we see ourselves as church leaders. We're not just overseers of programs, but we are a part of the Israel of God—the Church!

What I love most is the charge to reposition our thinking in such a way that we mobilize the ordinary. This shift in the way that we think requires us to see ourselves as missionary outreach overseers. This challenge moves us from functioning as elite professional ministers to practitioners who have one goal: the evangelization of the whole world.

Perhaps God will use this book to spark a small fire that turns the world right-side up for the sake of Christ."

Myron Pierce
Lead Pastor, Mission Church, Omaha
Church Marketing University

" The first Reformation put the Bible back in the hands of ordinary people. The current reformation is putting mission back in the hands of ordinary people. We know this has been God's intent for His people from the Upper Room until today. Ralph is one of my heroes and a practitioner who has equipped thousands of everyday people to live into their true inheritance as disciple-makers and leaders of simple expressions of the Church that can fill everyday spaces. We follow in his legacy in the Kansas City Underground, and this book will inspire and equip you to do the same. This reformation is unstoppable. Wise leaders will choose to be at the front end of this rising wave, rather than being left behind paddling in their own strength. Read this and get ready to ride this wave of the Spirit."

—Rob Wegner
Director, Kansas City Underground
Director, NewThing, North American Region
Director of Microchurch Next, Leadership Network

EQUIPPING EVERYDAY
MISSIONARIES
IN A POST-CHRISTIAN ERA

RALPH MOORE
RalphMoore.net

≡XPONENTIAL

Equipping Everyday Missionaries in a Post-Christian Era
Copyright © 2022 by Ralph Moore

Exponential is a growing movement of activists committed to the multiplication of healthy new churches. Exponential Resources spotlights actionable principles, ideas and solutions for the accelerated multiplication of healthy, reproducing faith communities. For more information, visit exponential.org.

ISBN: 978-1-62424-110-9 (paperback)
ISBN: 978-1-62424-111-6 (ebook)

Editor: Karen Cain
Cover Design: Art Speak Creative
Interior Design: Karis Pratt
Printed in the United States of America.

Revive.
Recharge.
Refresh.

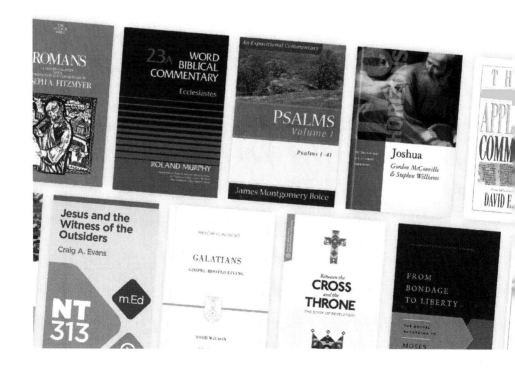

INSIDE

PROLOGUE

This is not the next great book on church growth, apologetics, or "soul winning."

It is neither an intellectual/apologetic or a "come to church" approach to evangelism. This book speaks to the needs of leaders who desire to equip their members to disciple others into Christ.

We've always preached "the priesthood of the believers," yet few of us live it with any measure of effectiveness. Though this priesthood addresses the needs of one another in the Church, we must also serve as "everyday missionaries" to the surrounding community. Today's America is a stewpot of self-identified people groups. To address each requires the effort of a host of everyday missionaries—ordinary people interacting with friends on a follow-me-as-I-follow-Christ journey.

What characterizes evangelism today is not a wrongheadedness about what needs doing. Instead, it parallels the disconnect between a hospital administration and its caregivers. The people leading the show have little direct contact with patients. The separation makes it difficult to understand their needs.

We present ourselves as servant leaders, yet we sometimes lord it over the flock. More often than not, we make evangelism about us and our programs. The purpose of this book is to flip the prevailing outreach paradigm on its head. The goal is for you to serve as an equipper, not as the lead evangelist. Your role is to prepare your people to live out and share their stories among their friends, neighbors, and enemies.

There are pockets of hope where this approach is working well. Obvious examples are Alan Hirsch, who taught us to value the forgotten ways. Francis Chan eschewed a megachurch for something closer to where people live. Brian Sanders, Rob Wegner, and Dave Ferguson lead healthy disciplemaking movements. Each of these people is a compelling example of a leader as an equipper. Many people heed these prophets among us. Others are pregnant with desire but unsure how to proceed.

This book is for those who struggle to implement what they watch others do well. A friend recently expressed a fear of "these new ideas of disciplemaking and church multiplication." Those "new" ideas have endured for two millennia. Yet they seem new to those trained in campus-centric congregations and program-driven evangelism.

Whenever you look at a fresh book, you need to determine whether it is a fit for you or a waste of your time. This one is no different. Let's start with what you won't get—another simple answer to complex problems. What you *will* find is an in-the-trenches approach to equipping your members do the work of an evangelist.

This book will aid you if you answer "yes" to any of the following questions:

- Do you struggle with motivating members toward evangelism?
- Does the surrounding culture threaten your attempts to grow *and* multiply the Church?

- Are you worried that lack of progress threatens your ability to fulfill your calling?

The book rethinks the axis between the pulpit and discipling mechanisms. These mechanisms exist in most churches. We'll assume that evangelism is primarily an "off-campus" endeavor. You'll learn to turn ordinary churchgoers into informal, everyday missionaries.

Today's post-Christian era is not unlike that faced by the first band of missionaries. They met an anti-Christian culture. Moral failures set them back. Finances were often in short supply. Like them, we serve among often complacent and sometimes divided and immoral members.

For us, a complication is "recentism." The tendency to cling to whatever worked in the recent past is a barrier to the future. The first-century Church struggled with recentism in its Judaistic tendencies. For us, evangelism has too long been defined as inviting someone to a church meeting.

For several decades campus-centered evangelism appeared to work best. Many imitated fast-growing churches that programmed evangelism into exciting events, need-meeting seminars, and Sunday services.

Today there is a tidal shift in North American churches. Attendance shrinks almost daily. Discouraged pastors quit in alarming numbers. What worked in recent years now fails most of us. We're awakening to understand that much church growth wasn't even growth. Select congregations added members while the "big-C" Church shrank. Much church growth was merely relocation of members from one congregation to another. Programming excellence attracted folks from other churches while attracting few new converts.

This reconfiguration is not new. Similar shifts occurred many times in the history of the Church. We must grasp the potential outcomes.

Tidal changes in church approaches either portend a long-term destructive future or an onramp to a spiritual awakening. The European Church in the 1950s slid into despair and loss after such a shift. Yet a parallel change in the U.S. Church in the late 1960s gave birth to an awakening we knew as the "Jesus People Movement."

Each major shift uncovers a chasm between approaches to church leadership. The widest rift ever was the Protestant Reformation. Ordinary people accessing Scripture in their spoken language precipitated a revolution. Today the difference is whether and how leaders equip their members for ministry. Church leaders either adapt to the Ephesians 4 APEST profile[1] or they don't. The results speak for themselves.

I walked through such a transformation during the 1960s and 1970s. Pastors I met while in college and during my tenure as a youth pastor reeked of despair. Tried-and-true evangelistic methods broke down at an alarming rate. Post-World War 2 church attendance peaked around 1956. Empty pews and church buildings turned into bars and art shops displaying the shift. What worked recently did—until it didn't.

The shift toward cultural irrelevance was fundamental and painful. But the Holy Spirit led past the misery into overflow. The transition toward an awakening felt like walking blindfolded through a furniture-filled room. The Church was adrift until ordinary, very young people took on the "work of an evangelist." They became everyday missionaries in places where pastors could not go.

Many leaders opposed the shift. They clung to church programs like attendance contests or "cradle-to-the-grave Sunday Schools." The reconfiguration introduced street evangelism, outdoor music festivals, and "love-ins" in parks. Older leaders who positioned themselves as servants to this counter-cultural movement undergirded it. They discipled young leaders who often possessed more enthusiasm than wisdom. The movement revitalized a stagnant Church.

Today the Jesus People Movement is mainly forgotten. Yet it morphed into the seeker-driven movement, which many hold dear.

It is time for another awakening. Recentism is an enemy causing many to cling to the past while the Spirit moves toward something new. The prevailing program-oriented church growth engine now sputters. It fueled mega and multisite congregations, but its attractional focus restricted it to adding numbers. It missed the opportunity to multiply churches and converts in succeeding generations. The dismal participation of Millennials and Gen-Z is proof of this.

We need a new operating system, not a new model. I hope to present one in these few pages.

The best success metric is our ability to equip our members to live as God's Ephesians 2 masterpieces. The past four decades molded these masterpieces into volunteers supporting church programs. We'll need to move beyond this inward-directed operating system to direct more attention to outsiders. We must prepare our members to serve as everyday missionaries where they live, work, and play.

In almost six decades of church leadership, I've watched thousands of non-believers come to Christ. Many departed the circle of our congregation to plant churches—sometimes on foreign soil. I can guide you toward similar results by utilizing simple Scriptural patterns.

Change is upon us, whether we like it or not. We now live in a post-Christian culture, one showing little respect for the gospel or for churches. You can choose business as usual. Doing so will result in further shrinkage of the "big-C" Church and stagnation in the one you lead. Or your church can become an effective instrument to bring the Kingdom of God to a hostile world.

How you position yourself as a leader is key to building and leading an effective operating system. Read on, and let's have some fun!

CHAPTER 1

A LESSON FROM THE BULRUSHES

You might compare an oppressed Church to the lot of Israel in the first two chapters of Exodus.

Egypt turned against a once-admired people. Political and physical restrictions dominated God's people. It was time for a change. That change came from unexpected sources.

Moses' mother and sister qualify as heroes, among others. They protected his life, as did the families of other male children. You might say they and others like them hoarded what God gave them. The king's daughter equipped Moses for life in the palace. Even before, the Holy Spirit worked through two Hebrew midwives, Shiphrah and Puah, who equipped Hebrew boys for life by sparing them. Only the king guarded the status quo, as his son and future king would also attempt (with disastrous results) when he met Moses and the Spirit of the Lord.

Security Guards, Hoarders, and Equippers

So, let's think of that ancient king as a *security guard* attempting to maintain a dynasty, the family as *hoarders* holding onto baby Moses, and the midwives and Pharaoh's daughter as *equippers* in God's grand saga. Each one fulfilled tiny bits of God's promise to Abraham made several centuries before.

We play small roles in the same tale. God created and gifted us as unique players in his remarkable story. We each have some say in the role we will play. Gifted indeed, but we control the gifts by our willingness to obey—or not.

Would you consider yourself a security guard, a hoarder, or an equipper?

You can describe most church leaders using one of these terms. We each feel the call to direct the flock God assigned us, but we each do that in our chosen manner.

Much depends on our spiritual gifts and our community. The availability of resources like money, talented people, or accessible meeting space contributes. Yet something very different *motivates* each leader: our personal view of the task before us.

Security Guards

Every human craves and seeks personal security, and church leaders are no exception. But play it safe as a security guard, and you lose the opportunity to reach your full potential. Tethering your members to yourself is like the king holding Israel from its destiny. Moses would have fit the profile of king if he'd built a mini-empire inside Egypt. That may have worked politically, but it would never have served God's plan for a nation free to bless the world.

Is your overriding instinct to protect your church from loss? Do you serve in a small community where young people escape to a city for better job opportunities? Are you assigned to a long-standing congregation of mostly retired folks? Do tight finances constrain you? Do you stand out as a minority in the community? The reasons for struggle abound. All these factors contribute to leading as a protector of the status quo. But doing so is a liability. It results in the loss of what you're attempting to protect.

Hoarders

No one wants to be labeled as a hoarder. Yet many of us hoard people, money, land, and other resources.

Hoarding can result from positive motivation. Moses' mother had good reason to hoard the lives of her sons. The hoarders among us may act from a desire to build the Kingdom and fulfill the Great Commission. They do this by adding to their numbers. But for some, this addition orientation is selfish at its root. The thinking may be, "If my church grows fast, I'll assume a measure of notoriety." The problem, of course, is that addition bows to multiplication. Our task is to make disciples who *go* rather than to collect spectators who *remain* tied to us.

Equippers

At the end of the day, the equipper best plays their small part in Jesus' royal pageant.

We should behave as Shiphrah and Puah did. Their decision to spare Hebrew children equipped Israel for the exit from slavery. These women lived in service to God's great purpose. They spared more boys than just Moses. They birthed an entire generation of male children. By the time Moses killed the Egyptian slave driver, there was a host of male Hebrews in his cohort. He would lead these men as fathers and grandfathers to the edge of the Promised Land.

Pharaoh's daughter took the raw material of an infant to new heights. We have little knowledge of what she did. We can deduce that her actions equipped Moses for leadership. Her role compares to a lead pastor enhancing the discipling efforts of individual church members. This attitude contrasts to pressing people into our programs.

You and I must equip our members—all our members—to act as spiritual midwives. Enlist them as volunteers, yes. But don't stop there! Prepare each one for their personal mission field. We must also equip select members to reproduce the congregation that nurtured them.

So, are you a security guard, hoarder, or equipper? The answer to that question depends on where your motivations lie.

CHAPTER 2

FORTRESS, FIELD, OR FORCE?

We must equip rather than manage, see opportunity in upheaval, and be about our Father's business. Anything less threatens our mission and falls short of presenting our bodies, positions, and possessions to God as a living sacrifice. The challenge to leaders is finding our place in this scary new world that largely rejects us and our gospel. This can't happen if we seek to replicate the past or hold onto what will never change. Every leader among us faces the same temptation to settle for comfort and a prize short of the goal.

Is personal peace and safety our primary concern? If so, we will opt for fortress-like security in our churches, buckling down and safeguarding the familiar with little actual sense of God's Kingdom on earth.

Do we seek significance in the eyes of our peers? This can set us up to look at church as a reflection of our ego—the bigger, the better. It is natural to want to be regarded as visible, reputable members of our communities. Respect is a big deal, but it can lead to the counterfeit goal of building a personal kingdom.

Are we willing to accept the Great Commission as a personal call? If the answer is yes, nothing will stand between us and spiritual revolution. Our treasures of time, money, and prestige will wreak with sacrifice. If the answer is no, nothing will really change at all.

You and I both crave the power of the Holy Spirit, hoping we can make a small difference in the world. If we embrace the goal of spiritual revolution, we can only be happy when leading a *force for change*. It will become easy to set aside comfortable traditions and patterns. This includes abandoning the program-based operating system of the last few decades. We must embrace a more mission-oriented system. Let's consider the recent past as an addition-focused OS or an "aOS" and the desired future as a multiplication-focused OS expressed as "mOS." Which will you pursue?

Trading the comfort of addition for the wild frontiers of multiplication is our only tenable avenue. Like Peter and Andrew, you and I must be willing to become "fishers of men" on a broad scale—and we must equip fellow fisherfolk to equip others as well.

Pandemic Insights

Throughout the pandemic, I watched a host of online sermons. Preachers are people I trust and respect. Two themes emerged. The first was that 2021 would be better than 2020. The second emphasized our "right" to hold indoor meetings, despite whatever we heard from the government or science.

Both strains appeared to long for the good old days of 2019, the year leading up to the disaster. Those leaders neglected to mention the "good old days" of AD 30–300 or the heroics of the Church in the face of the Black Death.

Many offered hope for the "new normal." I wondered whether the new norm would be to rest in Jesus or to *serve* him. We should think of evangelism wrapped in a cloak of love and service to others. Would this be a wake-up call to action, or would we simply slip back into what's comfortable?

As the crisis ended, most Church leaders felt disappointed. The Church shrunk. There was little talk about sending missionaries into the marketplace, let alone overseas. Evangelism was seldom discussed.

Watching multiple Bible teachers served as an informal survey. As a lurking spectator, I understood the need to comfort people in crisis. But simple comfort without challenge wasted leadership skills. The best-positioned equippers for evangelism were too worried about budgets and filling pews.

The crisis changed the Church. A third of attendees did not return to services. Many congregations no longer exist. There is much hand wringing about getting people back to the pews. The new normal is often hybrid, including online participation—and that's a good thing because it serves people who can't meet in person, including elderly members who can no longer make it to our buildings. The rest falls short of our calling.

We must rise to the situation like Ukraine rose to the threat of invasion. Let's examine three different ways leaders tend to position their congregations for spiritual warfare: as a fortress, a field, or a force.

Church as a Fortress

We can hunker down as though the church building and its programs are a fortress against the evil one. But this analogy presents a couple of problems. The first is that it confuses flesh-and-blood outsiders with our great foe, Satan. The second is immobility. While love motivates compassionate action, fear only leads to paralysis.

A fortress church seeks to provide an alternative to whatever the world offers. Efforts run the gamut. We provide safer Halloween events. We protect our young from the surrounding world with Christian schools and colleges. Christian counselors abound. None of these are wrong. Yet, a fortress mentality is a serious threat to the Great Commission.

I expect that the life of the Jerusalem church in its first couple of decades felt much like a fortress. Managing growth and persecution must have been difficult for the apostles. Whatever the reason, they disobeyed Jesus' commission. At least they did until Acts 8, about nine years into their history. Their self-protection further manifested when leaders feared meeting the converted Saul of Tarsus. They only engaged him after Barnabas' reassurance. Their efforts fell far short of making disciples to the ends of the earth (or even a few short miles away in Samaria).

Church as a Field

A church in my neighborhood displays a massive lighted billboard. It currently announces, "An invitation can change a life." I'm not sure most freeway denizens understand its meaning. The sign pollutes the minds of any church members whizzing past. Inviting someone to church is *not* evangelism, although invitations may accompany disciplemaking. I'm not throwing these people under the bus, but we must equip our members for more.

The Church is not a mission field. It never was.

A sign on a companion billboard reads, "No perfect people allowed." It is doubtful that freeway drivers gather much motivation from this slogan either. The earliest saints prevailed in a world where the neighbors would never dare to visit a church out of curiosity, perfect or otherwise. They knew that being a Jesus-follower meant being all in or all out. No sitting on the fence or feeling things out or keeping one foot in the door and one out.

Limiting your people to inviting others to events shortchanges them and the Holy Spirit. You need to prepare your members for the harvest. Offer them more than an opportunity to bid people to your performance. You see, the church as a mission field is a costly operation. A friend recently described church management as a seven-day hamster wheel. Staff and volunteers burn out while generating something new and more over-the-top each week. What does this cost in dollars that you could divert to more beneficial channels? What is it doing to your soul?

Church as a Force

Any paradigm other than your church as a missionary force sells you and your congregation short. It misses the mark of the call to make disciples of every nation.

The New Testament word *ethne* in the Great Commission addresses unique people groups. We often reduce it to a discussion of skin color or geography, but it is wider. Think of lifestyle or "identity groups" such as Pharisees, Sadducees, or Zealots when Jesus spoke. There were also trade guilds, publicans, and Roman soldiers. Each was set apart by self-identifiers and by community appraisal. Cultural diversity includes both racial and social/identity diversity. We must address *both* if we are to bring our world to Jesus.

Do you believe Paul's words in Ephesians 4? Our task is to equip ordinary Christ-followers as missionaries to the *ethne* around them. Do this well, and some will feel called away from your "Jerusalem" to far-flung localities and to the ends of the earth. And that's the real mission of the Church.

CHAPTER 3

TWO METAPHORS FOR EVANGELISM

One of my best friends came to Christ due to a conflict I had with his fiancé. She stopped speaking to me after I refused to perform her marriage to him, a nonbeliever.

The woman was a casual friend to my wife and myself. We'd helped walk her through a painful divorce and kept in touch at church gatherings and in her place of business. Our friendship took a hit when I refused to join her in an unequally yoked marriage. She quit the church.

She may have been unequally yoked, but she was equipped for evangelism. And the conflict over the wedding abetted the process.

In explaining her anger to her new husband, she touched on the gospel and the concept of an unequally yoked marriage. One day they showed up in church at her husband's insistence. His strong Jewish background and her commitment to Jesus found a home in my determination not to violate the Scripture. He became intrigued by a church willing to risk friendships because of its principles. Over time, he came to Christ and became a strong leader in the church. Today the two are among my dearest friends.

Many people in our post-Christian society distrust Christians, the Church, or God himself. They believe they know what we are about and have decided they don't want any part of it. Blame it on politicians, the media, or poor upbringing, but the reality is that we face a world not unlike that of the first-century Christians. This post-Christian era resembles the pre-Christian one.

How do we rebuild a bridge of trust? How do we develop spiritual friendships where genuine and transformational conversation can occur? Through ordinary believers invested in authentic friendships where love overcomes negative experiences and poor stereotypes. Let's look at two metaphors that help us understand how this kind of evangelism works.

A Path to Walk

The first metaphor is that of a path. Disciplemaking friendships are paths to walk rather than events to mark. The idea is to disciple someone into Christ rather than sell them a heavenly insurance package and hope to disciple them after the purchase.

An inward-focused congregation gets people to a church meeting or another event and then induces them to repeat a "sinner's prayer." After the decision to follow Christ, the church introduces a short training venue labeled "discipleship." Sometimes this includes more instruction on how to volunteer in the church than actual training in a person's walk with God.

Even a consumer-oriented church includes several gifted evangelists, as described in Ephesians 4. These folks will bring the event to the people, or they may disciple people into Jesus as I recommend. But a consumer-driven operating system does little to equip each member to disciple others into Christ.

I often wonder exactly at what point Matthew was born again. Was it when he walked away from his tax collector's shop? Was it when he put down his quill and stood from his desk to follow Jesus? Or was it when the reality of Jesus' miracles caught his attention and grew to allegiance?

Disciplemaking evangelism depicts each individual moving either toward or away from the Lord. That being the case, we must equip our members to nudge their acquaintances along the journey. This venture includes building solid Christian character rooted in trust and truthfulness.

If the goal is to be a wholehearted follower of Jesus, then we must realize that each person lives at different stages on the trek. The crucial question is whether we are moving in a fashion that inspires others to trust us.

Rebirth—a Process

The next metaphor of rebirth is explained in a conversation between Jesus and Nicodemus. Nicodemus came to Jesus with a series of religious questions. He questioned Jesus about who he was and how he operated. Jesus interrupted this quest for theological answers by informing Nicodemus of something he didn't understand: he needed to be born again.

So, let's investigate the metaphor Jesus used to describe entering God's Kingdom. The concept of being born again parallels our physical birth.

The process starts with conception. A seed of interest or trust finds its way into the heart of an individual who may or may not be seeking God. Maybe it is just a thought like, "This is a person I can trust— they're a Jesus person, but I trust them despite our differences."

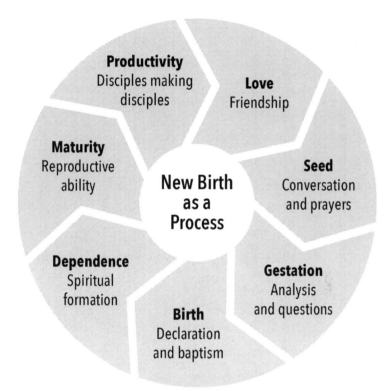

Productivity
Disciples making disciples

Love
Friendship

Maturity
Reproductive ability

New Birth as a Process

Seed
Conversation and prayers

Dependence
Spiritual formation

Gestation
Analysis and questions

Birth
Declaration and baptism

In the embryonic stage, the seed of faith takes shape. Still ill-formed, an individual's inner person begins to conform to the mind of Christ. On the outside, they may carry much baggage from their past life. Inside, they are growing toward a confessional relationship with Christ. This is where they admit their belief to themselves and then to the friend guiding them in their journey.

Gestation progresses to birth pangs. The person struggles with an awareness that they are processing an identity change. They question, "Is this real? Is it something I want to do?"

The new birth gives rise to a different identity. As in the physical realm, a born-again experience includes messy afterbirth. There are leftover wounds, hurts, and habits from the past. This afterbirth messiness may include conflict with non-believing friends and family.

Disciplemaking evangelism differs from event evangelism in many ways. The most important is that the person discipled into Christ is born into a new life possessing a basic understanding of spiritual realities. They possess the basic attributes necessary for life.

As babies, new Christians need coaching and support and a continued growth path toward maturity. The family of God is necessary; here is the place for a congregation to invest its resources. After someone is born again, they're going to question, "How do I know what I believe is real?" Apologetics, Christian terminology, and how to serve others are part of the maturation process. Classes and study groups are meaningful at this stage of growth. Knowledge gained must build on knowledge possessed.

The process of new birth, growth, and maturity begins by engaging someone who is not yet a Christian. It ultimately progresses to the possibility of serving as a missionary—possibly in another culture, but certainly each can begin as a missionary in their own backyard.

CHAPTER 4

EVERYDAY EVANGELISM

Growing up in church can be a disadvantage—at least when it comes to sharing our faith.

My youth pastor once asked me to give an eight-minute "sermon" to 120 of my peers in a high school event. Most people in the audience were either Christ-followers or bored kids whose parents dragged them to church. I naively decided to preach the gospel to them. The problem was that I couldn't find the gospel in the Gospels after reading all four of them. The writers never produced a gospel tract. They told a life-giving story.

There is neither the Romans Road nor any other concise gospel presentation in the Scripture, unless you include Peter's speech on Pentecost—at least I've never found it seven decades into my relationship with Jesus. My church programmed me to view the good news as a short sales pitch followed by a prayer to close the deal. (Such a prayer was another thing I never found in my Bible.)

I eventually discovered Christian apologetics and met with some success arguing friends into a decision to follow Jesus. But winning arguments wasn't very effective—and it is even less compelling in today's culture of non-linear thought.

What Does Work?

My friend Ed is the marketing director at a large medical lab in Hawaii. His social circle includes doctors and others in the medical community. Ed, two surgeons, and a biochemist met monthly in fancy wine bars. They batted around political views, work issues, and life in general. As a Christian, it was natural for Ed to speak about whatever God was doing in his life. He slowly gained the right to share his faith in Jesus.

As his pastor, I got invited to the group one evening. My buddy primed me to tell stories of my travels teaching about church multiplication in developing countries. A couple of years later, one of the surgeons showed up in church looking for Ed and me. His marriage was in crisis, and he wanted God in his life. That night, while sitting in a restaurant, Ed led the man in a prayer to receive Christ.

It turned out that our earlier conversation in the wine bar helped build a bridge with this man. He never mentioned it that night, but he had often served as a short-term medical missionary. The Spirit had built a bridge between us, as my ministry stories in other nations connected with his efforts in underserved nations.

The point of this account is that we're in this for the long haul, and we need to coach our people to build long-term friendships to reconcile their friends with their closest friend, the Lord Jesus Christ.

Avoid Arguments

Some of our members get burned by repeating a sermon or by inviting someone to church in a culture that deems churches and sermons irrelevant.

Some have lost arguments about science, evolution, and politics. Others encountered another person's fit of anger against God. Good people who want to spread the gospel sometimes suffer crippling fear of rejection. Not knowing how to handle possible backlash impedes living as an everyday missionary.

If you're trying to equip your members as laborers for the harvest, you might want to deconstruct evangelism into simple, ordinary conversations. Help your people understand they don't need to control discussions with not-yet believers to be effective. They will enjoy better results if they leave conversations open-ended.

Individual conversations are to another person's eternity as grains of sand are to a cement block: a bunch of them produce weighty outcomes, but any single one isn't a big deal.

I teach people to anticipate tough questions without allowing them to degenerate into arguments. The response to a question about God or the Bible they can't answer becomes, "I can't help with that because I don't have an answer. Let's you and I Google it or check Wikipedia and continue this conversation a week from today."

Teach your people to focus on loving others, building relationships, and remaining alert for natural points to interject God into their conversations. They will see progress through statements like, "I prayed, and this great 'coincidence' happened."

As soon as you remove the pressure people feel when attempting to control dialogue or sell something, they will begin to trust the Holy Spirit more than themselves. You'll be surprised by the results of simple friendship evangelism, where there is no need to close a deal or win an argument.

Sometimes people who seem least likely to accept Jesus become rabid evangelists. Those who are most effective at sharing faith are often the newest Christ-followers. They still live in the mission field and enjoy many friendships with pre-Christian friends. Effectiveness stems from a vocabulary free from churchy language coupled with fresh amazement at what Jesus did for them.

My friend Steven is an unchurchy, much-tattooed man—his body art includes his face. He recently gave a ride to a hitchhiking Marine so he could build a friendship pointing toward Christ. Bringing the young man home to Camp Pendleton got Steven into a bit of trouble. His expired driver's license and license plates got him arrested. Steven is a responsible person, both a personal trainer and real estate investor, so embarrassment piled onto his predicament. But he came away excited that he got to pray with three MPs during the ordeal. He also came away with a new friendship that he hopes will result in a new member of the Kingdom.

My own gospel-sharing goals are to *uncomplicate* things, speak in culturally appropriate terms, refrain from pressing anything, and live in patient expectation as the Holy Spirit draws people to Jesus. Embracing others in their cultural context beats hammering them with churchy words and expectations. Paul's example provides valuable wisdom for sharing faith:

> For though I am free from all, I have made myself a servant to all, that I might win more of them. To the Jews I became as a Jew, in order to win Jews. To those under the law I became as one under the law (though not being myself under the law) that I might win those under the law. To those outside the law I became as one outside the law (not being outside the law of God but under the law of Christ) that I might win those outside the law. To the weak I became weak, that I might win the weak. I have become all things to all people, that by all means I might save some. I do it all for the sake of the gospel, that I may share with them in its blessings (1 Corinthians 9:19-23, ESV).

Lighten up on your people, teach them to lighten up on their friends, and trust the Holy Spirit to turn seeds into fruit. Good times are just around the bend!

Give the Seed Time to Grow

My mother armed me with a trowel and a packet of carrot seeds one spring day. As a triumphant four-year-old farmer, I got the seeds in the ground, covered them with dirt, and did my bit with the garden hose. So far, so good! A day later, I dug up part of the tiny garden to check on its progress. Fortunately, my mom interrupted the premature harvest before I could ruin the entire project—and a couple of weeks later, we got to eat the fruit of my small labor.

I picked up a lot of missionary wisdom in a story Jesus told:

> This is what the kingdom of God is like. A man scatters seed on the ground. Night and day, whether he sleeps or gets up, the seed sprouts and grows, though he does not know how. All by itself, the soil produces grain—first the stalk, then the head, then the full kernel in the head. As soon as the grain is ripe, he puts the sickle to it because the harvest has come (Mark 4:26-29, NIV).

The farmer never digs up the seed to check for progress. He is patient. Growth occurs when he can neither see nor understand it, but he allows it without interference. Over time, he gets rewarded with the harvest.

The Holy Spirit works in the lives of individuals in ways that we cannot see and certainly cannot comprehend. Our job is simply to put the seed into the soil. Conversations can add water and fertilizer as we wait for the harvest. But we must remember that we're not alone. Paul described partnership in evangelism: "I planted, Apollos watered, but God gave the growth. So neither he who plants nor he who waters is anything, but only God who gives the growth" (1 Corinthians 3:6-7, ESV).

The Lord of the Harvest nurtures awareness of belief in the heart of a person coming to Jesus. Belief in Jesus brings someone into the Kingdom of God. As faith arises in them, they are born again.

Deep Hurts May Motivate Bad Theology

Christ-followers should remain patient with false theologies generated by popular music, superhero movies, and social media. A willingness to listen more than we talk is an operational asset.

We also need to prepare our members to accept some hostility in areas where a non-Christian person shows strong feelings. Coaching our people to sympathetically listen to the complaints (even tirades) of others is essential. Individuals will surface a wrong they heard about in the news media, which may parallel an evil done to them. The issue can appear as a question or challenge, "Why would a good God permit something like this?"

Rather than engage in an argument, we need to teach our members to offer empathy—hear the person out and possibly share personal stories of similar hurts and our lack of understanding of why this could happen. Ugly memories of a bad church experience are powerful obstacles to belief in God. Accusations against hypocrisy in the Church are lethal. An everyday missionary acknowledging the sad reality of hypocrisy can deflate these arguments. And the truth is that one hypocrite doesn't tar the entire family of God.

A good answer is always, "I don't understand this, and yet, here's what Jesus did in my life" or "I experienced a similar hurt." The point is to share the friend's anguish while bringing a measure of positivity into the conversation. We do not need to win arguments. It is critical to empathize toward eventual prayer opportunities.

Win Permission to Pray

Every human is a spiritual being. We all have a spiritual story to tell. Listening well while sharing similar stories destroys barriers and opens doors for the Holy Spirit to act in the life of another. When miracles happen, people pay attention. Better said, non-believers begin showing interest in God when prayer is mutual. Sometimes this can be defiant. After a Christ-follower prays with a non-believer, the person may look to Heaven with a challenge, "Are you going to act, or not?"

One of the most powerful things I did as a pastor was to teach church members to listen, empathize, and get to the point where they could ask a colleague, "Would it be all right if I prayed for you?" If the Christ-follower was shy, the script went something like, "You know I follow Christ, and I pray every night. Could I have permission to pray for you tonight before I go to sleep?" If they were bolder, the goal would be to pray together on the spot.

I still defer to this script several years after retiring from vocational pastoring. One neighbor, a house-flipper, struggled with a project that had been halted for many weeks due to a shortage of building inspectors. I asked if we could pray. He agreed, so we prayed while standing on the sidewalk in front of his house. An inspector showed up two days after we prayed. He was ecstatic to tell me about the answer to our prayers. Our relationship deepened when I later asked him to pray for me.

One of my friends recently got pretty fired up about this teaching. Naturally gregarious, he began praying with pretty much anyone he met. After praying with several acquaintances, he asked a mutual friend, "What should I do after I pray and God does what we asked?" Our buddy wisely answered, "After God does a miracle, you listen some more." An answer to prayer is less an invitation to preach than an open door to deeper conversations.

Hailing back to the parable in Mark, listening at this point reveals green shoots emerging in the soil of a human heart. After encountering answered prayer with a believer, pre-Christians begin to think a little differently about God than they did before. They will want to talk about the experience. Active listeners always win a hearing.

CHAPTER 5

SHIFTS THAT ARE CHANGING BEST PRACTICES

"The day of evangelism is over." At least that's what the speaker said. He was well-credentialed and moderately famous.

I was just a 24-year-old youth pastor in a small San Fernando Valley church, but his point shocked me into violent disagreement.

The speaker declared that the day of evangelism was past. In his mind, we needed to pursue personal sanctification in preparation for Christ's return. His was a fortress mentality. Yet, what the news media called the "Jesus People Movement" erupted over the next two years.

The Shift from Stasis to Jesus People

During the 1960s, sharing Christ with others was easy and effective. The day of evangelism never ended and won't until Christ returns.

Shortly after hearing this man spew his negativity, my wife and I planted a church in a small beach town. There were 12 of us on the first Sunday. In the next five decades, that dozen people multiplied into a movement. We were a disciplemaking culture from the beginning, encouraging small-group leaders who had multiplied their groups to plant new churches. Some were "one and done;" others multiplied churches that multiplied churches. A couple became megachurches. My proudest achievement is one string of church plants that went nine generations deep. The wonderful aspect is that every church planter came to know Christ through the church that launched them to plant another congregation. We now know of more than 2,600 churches worldwide that came about in spite of one man's opinion about the "day of evangelism."

We weren't alone. The so-called Jesus Movement spread across the world. Millions came to Christ while Christian "coffee houses" proliferated. Today we would call those coffee houses microchurches. Some grew into megachurches.

The movement was twofold in its approaches to evangelism. Concerts and marches paired with one-on-one relationships introduced people to Christ. The comingling of events and face-to-face encounters worked well.

Jesus music festivals and "love-ins" stoked momentum, but most evangelism was relational. The *Four Spiritual Laws* and *The Hollywood Free Paper* translated the gospel into street language. Answered prayer was a strong driver during the awakening. Instant deliverance from hard drugs, surprising healings, and other prayer miracles became common. A rebellious counterculture began to embrace the gospel.

The Shift from Jesus People to Consumer Church

The Jesus People Movement was joyous, but it only lasted for about a decade. Bible studies, sharing food with strangers in parks, and beach baptisms were changing the world. But suddenly they weren't. The revival ended. Churches once again required programs to support their members.

During the awakening, some of us (especially me) thought everything went well because we were wiser than our forebearers. When the revival ended, we finally understood it was a work of the Holy Spirit.

Shifts Affecting the Church and Its Mission	• 1930s "Christian America" • World War 2 (Deprivation) • 1950s Freedom, new social attitudes • 1960s Jesus People Movement • 1980s Consumer-driven church operating system • 2020s Pandemic and search for a new OS

The shift from the stasis of the 1950s into the Jesus People awakening was like the ocean tide rising upon a shore. The emergence from the Jesus People Movement was another tidal shift. It took us from easy spirituality into the consumer-driven church.

The Shift to a Post-Consumer Church

The shift to the post-consumer church is upon us, and it is painful.

First, a spiritual awakening brought the Church out of stasis and shrinkage. The second tidal shift led to two streams of ministry. The larger stream was consumer-driven, as many chose the seeker highway. The smaller stream focused on marketplace relationships. Money, or lack of it, sometimes dictated the difference.

The Consumer-Driven Operating System

The seeker-oriented congregations built consumer-driven strategies around an addition-focused operating system. Members functioned as salespersons inviting acquaintances to meetings where the pastor closed the deal. Small gatherings and training systems fed the beast. Often described as an inverted pyramid where the leaders served the members, the opposite was true. Individuals and small groups served the organization rather than the organization serving them.

The addition focus of the system reflected, at worst, a fear of loss. At best, it manifested strong growth in congregational attendance, financial health, and influence. Much good came of this, but the ability to rapidly multiply disciples who made disciples and to multiply churches that multiplied churches was mostly absent. The overwhelming influence of this operating system defines most evangelical churches today.

A Multiplication Orientation

Paralleling the seeker-driven movement, a more relational tilt emerged, driving congregations toward making disciples who could make disciples. These churches strove for multiplication rather than addition. There was, of course, overlap in styles. No church moved 100% in one direction to the total exclusion of the other. Consumer-driven congregations pulled evangelism *into* their Sunday services and other events. Multiplication-oriented churches saw evangelism as an everyday activity *away from* a church campus.

Disciples made disciples, often to the third and fourth generations. Churches planted churches with an eye toward "planting pregnant." In some situations, the multiplication went on for generations of new churches, and it crossed oceans. This activity was rare but culture-bending in many cases.

Programs and models aside, the difference was the operating system. A consumer-driven, addition-oriented operating system led to the Church as the mission field. A disciplemaking, multiplication-oriented operating system carried the gospel wherever its members went.

CHAPTER 6

CONSUMER-DRIVEN CHURCHES AND EVANGELISM

The consumer-driven operating system equips members to invite their friends to church meetings, youth activities, and to other programs. The members bring people to the church; the pastor's job is to get them into the Kingdom.

The power is in the program. If it is attractive enough, people will come. The words "We can do it; you can help!" define the consumer-driven system. The focus is inward. A pastor and staff are the primary players. The target audience displays spiritual hunger, or at least shows interest in attending church. The operating system consists of a bevy of programs, evangelism being its biggest one.

Addressing the Larger Culture

These churches play to felt needs in the communities they serve. There is a backstory to the emergence of the consumer-driven system. World War 2 changed the spiritual climate from what existed a couple of decades earlier. Americans made enormous sacrifices during the war. Emerging from the war and its horrid costs, the country also pushed off the Great Depression. American culture in the 1950s and 1960s showed little resemblance to that of the 1930s and 1940s.

People had more money. They enjoyed freedom from blackouts. There was no rationing of everything from tires to toothpaste. Families bought washing machines, and clothes dryers became more accepted. Advances in science and education promised a better, though more secular, world. Movies and television depicted new sexual freedoms. They also surfaced cultural depravity while bringing us idealized families to emulate. The message was about the viewer. The combination of influences generated a "me-centered" culture.

Immediately after the war, traditional churches increased in size and number. But they lost a measure of influence over the actions of their members. Then they lost members. The Jesus People Movement reversed this tide. Jesus movement leaders may have been hippies, but they became good event planners. The combination of a changing culture and talented leadership birthed the seeker churches. These new churches increased attendance and birthed influential congregations. They succeeded because they met the consumer-oriented needs of a self-oriented culture.

Boredom was an enemy. The Church focused on feelings of spiritual and psychological uplift. The attractional model worked to gather crowds. Adding numbers was a scorecard for success. Both strong Bible teaching centers and their more entertainment-oriented counterparts played the attraction game.

Confusing Church Growth with Evangelism

In mission-field churches, people get fed, uplifted, entertained, or all three. But remember, babies need feeding. Maturing children and adults feed and entertain themselves.

Church growth confuses itself with evangelism. Re-baptizing transfer members or baptizing our children can blind us to the shrinkage of the "big-C" Church.

Leaders often assume that if their church grows, they are doing most things right. Counting numbers is necessary, but not if we count the wrong numbers. Tracking the number of those who pray a 90-second prayer means little unless those people mature to reproduce disciples. Attending a membership meeting and volunteering to serve are practical measurements. But they are not as *effective* as measuring those making disciples outside the church.

The major weakness in the consumer-driven system is transfer growth. In 1990, George Barna published a book comparing the "big-C" Church to a large tree. He examined its roots and leaves. For Barna, the roots were smaller churches with little money and poor programming. But they were big on relationships. They had to build strong relationships because they lacked the resources to do much else. He observed that small relational churches bring more people to Christ than do large ones. In time, some of their members transfer to larger churches that offer great programs. Once relocated, they pray the prayer and check the boxes. The upshot is a game of musical chairs. Barna predicted this would destroy smaller congregations while confusing larger ones. In his prophetic scenario, the leaves would kill the roots, leaving the tree to wither and die.[2]

Barna's observations demand consideration. The emergence of massive congregations accompanied the decline of overall church attendance in America. The roots that fed the leaves and branches died fast enough to contribute to the general downfall. Our slice of the cultural pie shrank while we comforted ourselves with the growth of a few significant congregations. The consumer-driven, addition-oriented operating system failed us.

Unchurched Versus Evangelized

Unchurched Harry and Mary and similar metaphors came into our lives. They served as an easy way to help our members understand the power of an invitation to a need-meeting congregation. They were helpful until unintended consequences made a mess of things.

The term *unchurched* may equate to *unsaved*. But the word *churched* doesn't imply salvation. Toss in the idea of baby boomers returning to the church, and you see why the churched vs. unchurched paradigm inspired false hope. In many ways, the approach supplanted everyday marketplace conversations about Jesus. Getting someone into a church is not the same as actuating them as an operational member of God's family.

Harry and Mary took our eyes off the harvest, replacing it with a barn.

When Jesus spoke of a ripe, unharvested field, he wasn't only talking to 12 guys in ancient Israel. The inference is that all of God's creation needs a relationship with him. The harvest is ripe but often unnoticed.

I met one pastor who said his message and ministry only focused on certain people: those "who have a spiritual hunger they know Jesus can fill." He declared that he built every sermon around this narrow population. He further explained that nobody stays more than five years in his church. I attended one meeting when he demonstrated this. He asked the audience to stand "if you've been attending here for less than five years." Almost everyone in a crowd of about 1,000 people stood. He shocked me. The role of a pastor is to equip the saints to do the work of ministry, not to evangelize them himself.

None of this is to say that mission-field churches are not relational. Nor is everything they do built around seekers. But they operate from a program-centered, consumer-driven operating system. It is great for building a crowd but ineffective at winning the world to Christ.

CHAPTER 7

DISCIPLEMAKING AS EVANGELISM

In addition to seeker churches, another conduit emerging from the Jesus People Movement was a bent toward relational evangelism. Fewer churches pursued this avenue. Those that did often reproduced themselves. Those of us leading them often felt like prophets hollering in the wilderness.

This operating system is driven by disciplemaking. These congregations hold Sunday services and operate programs. There is a consumer element, but the operating system is different. They shift the focus toward members' unique giftings. These churches recruit volunteers. Yet they expect members to operate their gifts *away from* the church campus. Most programs and events aim to equip members for ministry instead of converting visitors.

The focus is on each member seeing themselves as a missionary to the world about them.

Everyday Missionaries

In churches that I pastored, we shifted from the events we ran during the Jesus People Movement to what we called "friendship evangelism." Today I would call it "disciplemaking as evangelism." That's cumbersome, but it describes our operating system. The idea is to disciple a person into Christ.

We assumed it is natural to share life on a follow-me-as-I-follow-Christ track. Call it what you will, but our goal was to turn each member of the body of Christ into a missionary. People would become "everyday missionaries," bringing the Kingdom of God into their very ordinary worlds. For the purpose of this book, I'll call this a disciplemaking operating system. We structured our church as a disciplemaking continuum, stretching from building friendships at one end to making disciples at the other.

We approached our members with an attitude suggesting, "You can do it; we can help." Or better put, "You can do it if we equip you for the task."

Biblical Simplicity

We stumbled on something approaching biblical simplicity. Our operating system meant discipling people into Christ while relying on the Holy Spirit for guidance and answers to prayer. This was key when praying with pre-Christians. We built our ministry and scorecard around how many people were being discipled at a given time. In turn, the goal was for those discipled into Christ to reproduce the process.

The new approach involves disciplemaking as a never-ending process. Disciplemaking begins before conversion. It continues in a friendship-based manner. Often an invitation to church or a missional community is the next step. The end goal is to equip the new Christ-follower to repeat the process. Our operating system tilts away from high-profile events to under-the-radar friendships. This approach prevails when evangelizing in a climate of hostility. It works among Buddhists in Hawaii and Japan. It works in post-Christian America.

Fewer Programs and Lower Costs

A surprising side benefit soon appeared. We emerged from the awakening of the 1970s with a return to programming, as did our seeker-oriented friends. However, as we built our strategies and structures around a different operating system, we found ourselves simplifying strategy, trimming programs, and spending money reproducing churches.

The need for vocational pastors (or the lead pastor as a counselor) bowed to our disciplemaking circles. Youth programs took form as a cluster of disciplemaking circles. Evangelistic events hardly existed— we even treated Easter as a normal weekend service so the once-a-year attendees would get a dose of the real thing. There was no need for an "outreach pastor" or a director of missions. Most ministries began as a bottom-up emergence from our everyday missionaries and the opportunities they surfaced.

What I've just described allowed us to operate with a smaller staff. We were able to stack church services across a weekend, hosting as many as seven "Sunday morning services" between Friday and Sunday evenings. Taking a disciplemaking approach to worship bands meant that a less-skilled member might play an unplugged instrument until they caught up with the rest of the band. Disciplemaking even the programs we did host freed us to build new crews for each service—no worship leader played in more than one band. No children's worker served in more than one service.

The savings in overhead costs freed funds for church planting. And it equipped us to send well-trained teams whenever we launched a new church. During my tenure as pastor, we attempted to plant churches of around 150 people on launch day. Some were larger. Those in far-flung places took smaller core teams. Today I would take a different tack by multiplying most new congregations as microchurches, adding funding and other resources as growth or rapid reproduction called for it. But, while discussing reduced costs in this model, I am proud that three times we launched churches by releasing more than 20% of our congregation to nearby towns. One Sunday, we planted two congregations with more than 25% of our people departing.

The operating system did have an attractional side to it. Each time we sent a group to plant a church, our attendance took a hit. But we would see those numbers replaced within weeks. It seemed that bored believers were attracted to the action. And our everyday missionaries somehow benefitted, in that their pre-believing friends wanted to know more about what we were doing.

CHAPTER 8

METAPHORS FOR EVERYDAY MISSIONARIES

Americans tend to overcomplicate things. I know because I am an American. We prefer splashy events to quiet friendships as strategies for bringing people to Christ. Yet Jesus taught us that we are salt and light in a hurting and often hostile world. Salt and light don't make a lot of noise. They achieve their purpose without attracting much attention. Biblical metaphors for disciplemakers are much the same.

Fisherfolk

The first metaphor is of fishermen. Perhaps it is more correct to say "fisherfolk." Jesus launched public ministry by calling people to grow into fishers of men and women. The men he called knew how to catch fish. He would disciple them to become fishers of people.

In this metaphor, we go where the fish are, rather than calling them to the shore. We must teach our people to spend time where the fishing is good. This may require cutting back commitments to church activities and spending time with friends and acquaintances outside the church, where the fishing is good.

We should train our people to spend time with people who seem to be hurting. And we should alert them to Holy Spirit-generated opportunities for friendships to blossom. This may call for a restructuring of Church life away from an overload of time-consuming busyness. We must make way for more time spent making disciples of outsiders.

I recently visited a vibrant small group attached to a healthy church. These people love Jesus and each other. But I was saddened when they discussed the pastor's sermon about serving others. Every response suggested serving within the circle of their congregation. No one mentioned a friend or neighbor outside the church family. The group is too congregation-centric to address the call of the Great Commission. Their leaders need to shift the focus from inward support to outward mission. Doing so will affect their schedule and program load. How about you and your congregation? Do you need to rethink these things?

Reconcilers

My wife and I spent eight years estranged from someone dear to us. Then a third party came into the picture. A total outsider to the separation, this person took it upon themselves to bring us together. The effort bore immediate and joyous fruit in all our lives. This person was a Holy Spirit-inspired reconciler who helped us tunnel through a massive wall of separation.

We should help people see themselves as *reconcilers* between friends. To bring your friend at work into friendship with your friend Jesus is reconciliation at its finest.

Paul described each Christ-follower as a new creation (born again); he depicted the Father reconciling the world to himself. Paul continues the mechanics of reconciliation when he says the Lord delivered this message of reconciliation to *us*. We are the reconcilers in partnership with the Holy Spirit in this word picture.

I've heard my friend Dave Ferguson say, "I want to help people *find their way back* to God" (emphasis added). Hundreds of conversations have convinced me that the Spirit shows himself to every child early in life. The wonder of those early moments gets lost as we grow up amidst negative spiritual influences. These early God-encounters may explain our culture's interest in the superpower and supernatural aspect of many video games and movies. It's our job to re-introduce our friends to their greatest friend, Jesus, who died to restore them to their Heavenly Father.

The task is easier if it remains informal. Our job as evangelists doesn't include preachiness. It's not our responsibility to make a convert or close a sales call. The task includes helping others realize there is a God who has positive intentions for them. It asks us to extract whatever positivity toward God is in them. Scripture teaches that God has revealed himself to every creature. As they begin to speak of the positive things in their life—them, not the disciplemaker talking—they grow in spiritual awareness. It's not difficult to reconcile men and women to a God who loves them. But you must begin with the things the Holy Spirit has already put in their hearts. You can build on their responses to those God encounters. Many nonbelievers will discover that they already have positive sentiments toward God. Building on those responses gradually moves people into reconciliation with God through Jesus.

This is more than theory:

> For when Gentiles, who do not have the law, by nature do what
> the law requires, they are a law to themselves, even though they
> do not have the law. They show that the work of the law is

written on their hearts, while their conscience also bears witness (Romans 2:14-15, ESV).

God gave evidence of his interaction with every human in the Old Testament: "Yet God has made everything beautiful for its own time. He has planted eternity in the human heart" (Ecclesiastes 3:11, NLT).

Marathon Runners

I met Bill on my first day of high school. Four years passed before he prayed to invite Jesus into his heart. This was just two weeks before graduation. Our prayer occurred on a sidewalk as we walked to our after-school jobs. You could compare the time in between to a marathon or cross-country race.

He was a jock; I was not. We were often together in the same classes. From time to time, I could bring my faith into our conversations, especially when he had problems at home. We prayed together on several occasions. We spent time together on sunny days as we'd walk the two miles from school to work.

After several years of running this race, I led him in a kid-level prayer to invite Christ into his life. The race had been long. I wouldn't have said I discipled him into Christ, but that's what happened. As we ran the course called high school, my friend came to follow me as I followed Christ. Our talks about life, its frustrations, and God were a marathon that ended well.

Paul capped his life experience by saying, "I finished the race." He advised the church in Corinth,

> Do you not know that in a race all the runners run, but only one gets the prize? Run in such a way as to get the prize. Everyone who competes in the games goes into strict training. They do it to get a crown that will not last, but we do it to get a crown that will last forever (1 Corinthians 9:24-25, NIV).

Paul's exhortation is that we should be as focused and dedicated as those runners in popular ancient games. Our motivation in serving Christ is much higher; we "run" not for a temporary crown but for an eternal one.

In Philippians, Paul reminded us that only one runner wins in a race. However, in the Christian "race," everyone who pays the price of diligent training for the cause of Christ can win. We don't compete against one another or even for church growth. The prize will appear when we hear, "Well done, good and faithful servant."

CHAPTER 9

THE ANSWER TO ANTI-EVANGELISM

America is in a sea of change regarding Christianity and evangelism. Some term us "cultural imperialists." Opinion pieces in the media call us out for imposing our political views on others. Unfortunately, some Christians underscore the media attacks by contributing to the political polarization of our country. We blunt our swords by adding to the division rather than piercing souls with the love of Jesus. Churches are finding that what worked in the past isn't working anymore.

How Good News Goes Bad

Outside the Church, evangelism has never been popular. The gospel as a disruptor put the Church at odds with large financial interests as far back as the colonization of North America. Opposition was international during the expansion of colonization across the world. Biblical values of freedom and human dignity stood in stark contrast to slavery and labor exploitation. But the problem persists and is growing in post-Christian America.

Today's TV talking heads don't help our efforts. Christians get stereotyped as salespeople peddling a product that doesn't interest our "victims." Too often, this is true. It can feel like we're trying to remove people from a lifestyle already providing them with an identity and purpose. And today's climate of identity politics precludes most discussions of moral absolutes. We need a different way into the hearts of needy people.

Perhaps our biggest failures stem from the perception of salvation as an event rather than a process. We produce an argument or sales pitch and then close the deal with a spiritual transaction. The result is a sign-on-the-dotted-line mentality. That affects our members, as it pressures the salesperson while eliciting shallow decisions from those who commit.

Jesus never asked us to convert people. He did command us to make disciples.

Disciplemaking involves a host of informal, often unconscious, paradigm shifts. These lead to a more formal transaction: baptism. Baptism is the public declaration we find in the New Testament. However, baptism occurs *after* engagement with God. It is aided by another human alongside the ever-present activity of the Holy Spirit.

War or Diplomacy?

Evangelism can feel more like war than diplomacy. Outsiders grow angry when they perceive Christ-followers, or anybody else, trying to push something onto them they don't want.

For years, churches taught members to approach evangelistic attempts as battles to win rather than friendships to build. This is futile. It frightens our members and angers the people we want to reach with good news about God and his love.

People inside the Church feel put off by the surrounding culture. They assume they must do battle to "win" someone to Christ. The result is that they either shrink back from any mention of Christ or set about winning arguments. The warfare approach requires having apologetics down cold and being ready with answers to every possible challenge.

If you're into warfare, you better equip your people to have their guns ready. If not adequately armed, you'll frighten them into silence. And if you do arm them, they're probably just going to anger others. Even so, the mission as warfare results in shaky success.

Love, Acceptance, and Forgiveness

The world we live in cries out for tolerance. Jesus calls us to love our neighbors. We must hold to our values and moral positions while loving those who stand against them. Doing so means we cannot prove ourselves unloving of others. As believers in a broken world, we walk a tightrope as we balance biblical values with love for those not holding them.

I got to pray with a Muslim friend for God to bless his business "as Jesus taught us to pray." He thanked me repeatedly for praying. A couple of days later, he prayed that Allah would bless me and my family. I responded by praying that Allah would bless him and his family.

So how do I justify such a prayer? Christians in Muslim lands must sometimes sue their governments to be able to call the God of the Bible "Allah." It is the name understood by their Muslim neighbors. I figure if that name works for them, it works for me. I'm building a discipling relationship with an acquaintance who serves Allah while remaining open to prayers in Jesus' name.

Love and good deeds can melt political and social barriers. An individual displaying love for another can take the gospel of love, acceptance, and forgiveness where events and marketing schemes cannot. Those who resent our public attempts at spreading the gospel will grow to accept it in small bites in the life of a devoted friend.

Think of making disciples of unbelievers as a quiet, invasive process. Contrast this operating system to a full-scale attack implied by other game plans.

Friendmaking Precedes Disciplemaking

Friends rub off on each other. This follow-me-as-I-follow-Christ approach makes stronger disciples than the consumer conversions followed by a series of classes on discipleship.

Friendship comes before discipleship, so friendmaking precedes disciplemaking. Our job is to equip people with spiritual insights into the process. We must help our members understand how sharing life can lead to prayer and spiritual discussions—all without manipulating others or becoming cultural imperialists.

We're not here to change people's political beliefs. We're not even called to change their behaviors. Sanctification is the Holy Spirit's job, and we should never usurp it.

Keep On Keeping On

Church attendance is shrinking. Programs are less effective than before. And negative press abounds. Some Christian leaders propose dropping evangelism altogether. One friend spoke to six pastors in his city, asking each what their church did to spur evangelism. All gave the same basic reply: nothing.

I've encountered Christian leaders who suggest that we see ourselves as unifiers of our communities, not evangelists. They endorse offering social blessings and programs to elevate the downtrodden. They have recast the Great Commission as something other than evangelism. Community uplift is necessary, and our churches must be at the forefront. But community development falls short of bringing people to know Jesus unless it includes building disciplemaking friendships. Social impact without spiritual transformation takes us off point. Anything other than equipping our members to make disciples is severe mission drift, which leads to the ultimate abandonment of the Great Commission.

Troy Evans and Myron Pierce lead disciplemaking congregations in underserved communities in Grand Rapids and Omaha. Both lead multiple efforts to improve the health, financial condition, and hireability of their constituents.

Troy makes disciples who make disciples and plant churches while leading a church called The Edge and a community development agency called Rapid Growth.[3] Myron leads Mission Church in Omaha while heading up Hope Houses, which transition people from prison into the working community. A companion ministry is called Shift Omaha. It teaches entrepreneurial skills and helps people start businesses with skills they already possess.[4] Both men are among the most effective community builders I've met. They do this wholeheartedly while equipping their members and volunteers to make friends and make disciples. They have unlocked the secret of "both/and."

So how do you perceive your role as a Church leader? Does your job description center on building helpful programs and managing Sunday extravaganzas? Is your purpose to preach sermons aimed at evangelizing people in your building? Are you a protector of the oppressed? Or are you bent on equipping God's people to live as everyday missionaries in the ordinary course of life?

CHAPTER 10

NEW TESTAMENT ROLE MODELS

C hurch "how-to" books can be confusing. Everyone has a different model that worked for them, and much ink is spilled over congregations appearing relevant to current culture. I may be offering a similar quick how-to without realizing it. But I hope to use the New Testament as my starting point for the marathon called evangelism. It presents an operating system that can support a variety of models in a multiplicity of times and cultures.

Jesus Begins with Friendship

We'll begin with Jesus; we can't call his example a marathon. It's more like a three-year sprint. However, Jesus still displayed friendship evangelism. We'll restrict this to the incident at the well in Samaria as recorded in John 4.

First, Jesus involved himself with a stranger from a different people group. Ask yourself who spoke first, Jesus or the woman? Not only did Jesus initiate the conversation, but he overcame both racial prejudice and misogyny by talking with a Samaritan woman in public. He was willing to drink from her cup.

Second, he aroused her spiritual curiosity. Rather than preaching, he threw in a confusing spiritual truth, "If you knew the gift of God and who it is that asks you for a drink, you would have asked him and he would have given you living water" (John 4:10, NIV).

Third, he invoked the supernatural when he displayed his knowledge of her history with men.

The fourth move was when he revealed the inadequacy of people's attempts to reach God and began to show a better way to the Father.

We don't know how long Jesus remained in Samaria, but his short visit with this "person of peace" brought new life to an entire village. The process was compacted, but it illustrates steps we can take to bring a friend into a relationship with God.

Paul Searches Out Hungry People

We're familiar with Paul's strategy of seeking hungry people in synagogues. But let's examine Acts 16 and the account of his brief stint in Philippi for more expanded evangelistic tactics.

First, he sought out spiritually hungry people gathering near a river. People into New Age spirituality or other fringe religious perspectives come to mind.

Second, his tactic was to dialogue with these people, harvesting an ongoing friendship—a friendship that grew into a significant church.

Third, he invoked the power of the Spirit when he freed the demonized girl.

Fourth, he was opportunistic. Illegally thrown into jail, he and his companions remained in place when an earthquake might have liberated them. The jailer, who believed he'd lost his prisoners, was poised to attempt suicide, but Paul interrupted him, building a short relationship with him and baptizing the man and his family that night.

(Please note this near instantaneous conversion serves as the exception to my argument favoring friendship evangelism—or it proves that friendship might not always be an elongated process.)

Fifth, he stood his ground. Paul and Silas refused to leave the jail until their accusers apologetically escorted them from the prison. An act of measured civil disobedience would have given courage to the fledgling group of believers.

The sixth step was when Paul gathered his friends before leaving town. I see this as introducing new believers to one another, providing the essential relationship necessary to birth a church.

Philip Partners with the Holy Spirit

We meet Philip as a deacon serving tables early in Acts. Judging from the numbers depicted earlier, he must have overseen the labor of other people. This would place him in a position of recognized leadership.

Whatever the case, we encounter him as an evangelist only after persecution forces him and others to flee the comfort of their home church for less-familiar circumstances. He carries a Greek name, so Samaria may have felt more at home to him than to his Jewish brothers and sisters. Either way, he begins evangelistic ministry as a preacher, which is something most ordinary Christians would not. The New Testament later described him as an *evangelist*—I'm thinking of Ephesians 4 when I read that term.

At any rate, we read in Acts 8 that Philip followed the Spirit's lead by heading toward the road from Jerusalem to Gaza. Along the way, he encountered an Ethiopian official who showed interest in the Hebrew Scriptures. The rest is history.

But the picture is of a man willing to follow the lead of the Spirit and step across racial and national boundaries with their attendant prejudices. He preached an incomplete gospel in Samaria, requiring the correction of Peter and John. But he was willing to get out of himself and take whatever seemed the correct path to follow.

From these examples, friendship evangelism flies under the radar in cultures hostile to the gospel. Our goal is to gather scriptural tools for equipping our people as everyday missionaries to their acquaintances and the subcultures where they operate.

Everyday missions don't always require much time to be effective. One friend, a 68-year-old woman, tells of bringing a man to Christ on a three-hour flight. The man said his sister had been "working on him" for years, but my friend explained the gospel in a way that made sense. These two women partnered in the gospel without knowing each other. The one was in for the long haul, while the other (probably an Ephesians 4 evangelist) capped off the journey in a few hours.

CHAPTER 11

UNDERSTANDING EVERYDAY MISSIONARIES

Jim was a well-schooled engineer and evangelical Christian, conservative in his attitudes, dress, and demeanor. Aaron, his workmate, was his opposite in many ways. He was a B-student who dropped out of high school just before graduation to devote his life to surfing and motorcycles. Eventually, he landed an engineering job because of his skills in hot-rodding motorcycles. He surfed, dabbled in drugs, and had a reputation for chasing women. The intersection of their lives would change a culture.

The unlikely friendship reached a pinnacle on the day Aaron had planned to commit suicide. He meticulously picked a time and place and purchased the drugs for an overdose.

Not knowing of the suicide plan, that afternoon, Jim (who had previously shared life, stories, and bits about Jesus) gave Aaron a small paperback copy of Paul's letter to the Romans. Aaron says he spent nearly an hour reading the book while hiding in a workplace restroom. He also says he didn't understand any of it, but it had him in tears.

Unable to understand his emotions, Aaron asked Jim to go for a drive after work. Jim explained the presence of the Holy Spirit. Parked alongside a highway, Aaron was born again. His new life in Christ began at almost the exact time he had planned for his life on earth to end.

Jim's next move was to bring Aaron to our fledgling church, where he would find people who fit his identity profile. In reaching out to Aaron, Jim had crossed into a social tribe quite removed from his own. The pair shared engineering interests but had little else in common. Respecting their different tastes, Jim realized that bringing Aaron to Jim's liturgical church would have stunted the new life inside him. Jim was an everyday missionary using friendship to cross boundaries and touch people otherwise uninterested in the gospel.

Upon embracing Christ, Aaron embarked on a rampage of restitution with anyone he had wronged in his past. His Jesus mania cost him his girlfriend, although someone else later brought her to Christ. Today they are happily married with grandchildren. A natural leader, it was Aaron Suzuki, his family, and mine who spearheaded church-planting in Hawaii. Jim Doehla's friendship evangelism bore fruit in ways he could never have imagined.

Everyday missionaries build intentional friendships across social boundaries—like Jesus and the woman in Samaria, Paul and the God-fearers he spent time with, and Philip in both Samaria and on the road to Gaza. Like Jim and his friendship with Aaron. Like my actor friend who left the suburbs to live as a missionary in a run-down area of urban Los Angeles. Missionaries cross cultural boundaries to expand the Kingdom of God—everyday missionaries do the same thing, just closer to home.

A Different Kind of Missionary

Harriet Tubman is often called "Black Moses" because of her efforts to deliver others from slavery after her escape. Not satisfied with rejoicing in her victory, she maximized it with 19 trips into the South, rescuing at least 300 enslaved people.

Tubman was raised into slavery in eastern Maryland in 1822, escaping to the North in 1849, 14 dangerous years before the Emancipation Proclamation. She later described her efforts on the Underground Railroad by saying, "I never lost a passenger." Fellow abolitionists portrayed her faith in God as the source of her strength. She said, "I always tole God 'I'm gwine [going] to hole stiddy on you, an you've got to see me through.'" Her record is even more dramatic because she lived with a $40,000 reward posted for her capture. A believer, and a different kind of missionary, her courageous life serves as a template for people delivered from Satan's grasp who cross back into the world they escaped, hoping to free others.

On her dangerous missions, Tubman first had to convince slaves that they could trust her. After that, she could invite them to accompany her on the obstacle-ridden journey to freedom. Some of those rescued by Harriet Tubman reproduced her efforts by saving others. Our mission is much the same.

Peter touched on this when he depicted believers as "sojourners and exiles" just after pronouncing them "a people for his own possession, that you may proclaim the excellencies of him who called you out of darkness into his marvelous light" (1 Peter 2:9-11, ESV). We who have been delivered live as foreigners in a culture without Christ, crossing the ever-present barrier to a non-Christian world. Our job as equippers is to help members reorient their identity around the Great Commission, ultimately equipping them to function as everyday missionaries.

A Prayer for Labor

My goal as a pastor was to equip every member to gather the capacity of those unnamed believers in Act 11. After fleeing persecution in fear, they established at least two congregations when they got to Antioch—one encompassing Jews only and the other open to Gentiles. I look at every individual through this lens. My perpetual prayer for labor for the harvest focused on turning an oft-quoted but seldom realized slogan, "Every member a missionary," into reality in our congregation. Disciplemaking at full throttle potentially transforms agnostics into disciplemaking missionaries to other nations. As a pastor, I would look at each new believer as a potential missionary to Japan. Obviously, most never made it there, but they discovered an effective missionary role somewhere between the front door of our church building and the mission field.

CHAPTER 12

OVERCOMING CULTURAL BARRIERS

Several decades ago, missionary author Ralph Winter identified three levels of evangelism, each distinguished by the cultural distance between the speaker and the hearer of the gospel.

When we teach our people to recognize the cultural distances between themselves and other community members, the importance of personal relationships becomes apparent. Winter described these cultural gaps as E1, E2, and E3. I add E0 and teach that each gap includes a barrier that we might call B1, etc.

People falling into the E0/B0 category are members of your church or people who may transfer from another to join with you. Cultural Christians or even backsliders fall into this category because there is no cultural gap or barrier between you and them. You share base values, a common language, and even an understanding of "churchspeak."

E1 Missionary Efforts

E1 includes your neighbor who doesn't believe in Jesus but who reflects your particular cultural identity. It includes members of your socioeconomic strata. These people eat what you eat and enjoy recreational activities similar to yours while holding no apparent relationship with God through Christ.

The barrier is their worldview; they may be atheists, agnostics, or people who simply never paid much attention to Christian things. The divide is real but not as significant as E2 or E3. Evangelism is easiest here, as there is only one spiritual barrier between you and them. Philip bringing Nathanael to meet Jesus is an excellent example of E1 evangelism.

E2 Missionary Efforts

E2 individuals are culturally different from the person sharing faith. Significantly, this person *self-identifies* with a people group dissimilar to the person reaching across the barrier. They may be from an immigrant culture, reflecting a unique religious outlook. They may entangle their personal identity with a sport or a social cause. Sexual identity is a formidable barrier. As a student of window stickers on other people's cars, I've noticed that pet ownership is now an American identity group. We can't avoid social justice warriors either. Each is a tribe with its own set of social morals and prejudices.

The two barriers are the differences in lifestyle coupled with the worldview barrier. Evangelism is more complicated—add lifestyle politics to the mix, and the fences grow taller. Crossing these barriers is slow and sometimes painful. It can be more fruitful when the person coming to Christ enjoys influence in their identity group. They function as the person of peace Jesus described in Luke 10. The Samaritan woman in John 4 was E2 to Jesus, certainly to his disciples, but she became an E1 missionary to her village.

E3 Missionary Efforts

E3 reflects a recent immigrant from a radically different culture and worldview. My Islamic physician fits into this category, as would someone you would meet on a mission trip to another country.

A team you send to plant a church on foreign soil encounters E3 evangelism.

This is where evangelism is most difficult, and relationship-building demands patience. Here a person spreading the gospel encounters a worldview barrier, significant lifestyle differences, and a linguistic barrier. These are people of very different cultures from those who extend the gospel to them.

Penetrating Cultural Barriers

When equipping our members to build friendships across cultural barriers, we need to help them appraise what is vital to the culture of the person they've befriended. Everyone is a microcosm of their own culture. Each identifiable cultural difference also reflects a barrier to overcome if they would introduce an individual to Christ. Penetrating each barrier takes longer and requires more unwavering love and friendship.

It's easiest to cross the social barrier by accepting an individual just as they are. A requisite willingness to understand another person's values doesn't mean buying into them. The natural flow of friendship, identifying with another person as they unveil life's problems and challenges, rounds out the picture. An everyday missionary moves toward sharing faith by linking their life history with their friend's story.

What Is Good News to This Culture?

We need to train our members to ask, "What is good news in the culture we hope to address?" Also, "What would be good news to the person we befriend?" "Where do they find meaning?" "What brings them joy?" "Where do they hurt?" Life's central issues are a part of every person's psyche, and they transcend culture. They are the pathways into a human heart and mind.

After identifying significant issues in another person's life, we start to think about story-linking. How can I relate my story to their story? How can Jesus' stories weave into our conversations in ways this person might value? Where do the stories of Jesus connect to the stories in my friend's background?

Questions like these shape human lives. They craft a roadmap into the lives of others. Each human is different from every other, but there are similar needs in the heart of every person.

Where Does This Culture Feel Pain?

We know that Paul's missionary efforts centered on Western Turkey and Greece. We also understand that these cultures demeaned women. Misogyny was a point of pain then as now.

Luke wrote that everyone in Asia heard the gospel because of Paul's disciplemaking efforts in Ephesus. Paul demonstrated respect toward women. The apostle John focused attention on Jesus' healthy relationships with women in his Gospel. Many people view John's writing as a successful attempt to undergird the movement in Asia. Linking John's Gospel with Paul's efforts, we see unity in the apostles' attempts to bring healing to pain in a culture.

Paul's admonition to slaveholders is another example of Christian values addressing and undermining a source of pain in pursuit of the Great Commission. Bible narratives are meaningful when addressing similar wrongs in people's minds today.

How Does This Person See the Spiritual Realm?

For many years I have coached church planters in Japan. Theirs is a culture of shame more than guilt.

Westerners respond to the cross via the forgiveness Christ makes available. People in the Japanese culture initially open their hearts to a person who leads with Scriptures addressing shame. Japanese people understand the spiritual world and quickly respond to teaching that touches on demonic activity and spiritual warfare. Japan is a secular nation on the surface, but individuals deal with deep spiritual issues. Many people dedicate their children to spirits at Shinto shrines, and Japanese folklore is replete with evil spirits often seen as tricksters.

As a perpetual short-term missionary to Japan, it took a long time before I understood these factors. The problem was mine. I knew that my friends saw the world differently from me, so I learned to eat new foods, remove my shoes when entering a home, and bow rather than offer a handshake. Yet, more than a decade of close friendship with leaders passed before I began to understand (if I do yet) their view of the spiritual realm.

If we're training and equipping our members for evangelism, we need to help them recognize how others view the spiritual universe. It's often a cobbled-together theology born of social media or action movies. In reality, these and similar factors shape the theology of the American mission field. Politeness suggests that if you listen to their theology or their stories, they will listen to yours.

CHAPTER 13

BLENDING FRIENDMAKING AND DISCIPLEMAKING

I once encountered a European vocational missionary *bragging* about his (shallow) accomplishments. Every day several people greeted him on the bike path he took daily to a favorite coffee shop. On arrival each day, he met with other missionaries in the coffee shop— hardly adequate after two years in the country. This man sadly seemed unable to venture across cultural boundaries to engage the people he hoped to reach. Instead, he was content to drive past them in order to sit across the table from people with whom he felt more at ease.

Contrast that story with Dustin Nelson and his wife. Feeling called to plant a church in Southern California, these two school-teachers moved from Florida without knowing anyone in the area. They met Ryan Delameter, leader of a group of bivocational pastors planting after-hours churches in coffee shops. (These OCNWTR [ocean water] churches also provide water treatment systems to over-seas communities. Check out ocnwtr.com for the full story.)

Ryan challenged the Nelsons to start their new church in a coffee shop or on a beach. They chose the beach in Oceanside, California. The first "Jesus Party" consisted of four people, a guitar, s'mores, and hotdogs. Soon this small group was making friends of strangers. The food played a large part in building intentional friendships. These churches are small, numbering around 40 members each, but Jesus Parties have been planted in the original Oceanside location, Malibu, Catalina Island, San Clemente, and two more in Oceanside. Most of their growth comes from the religious "nones" and "dones." Jesus Parties run on an mOS that touches people unreached by the rest of the evangelical community.

But what about *our* people? Do they build intentional friendships? Do they seek those on the fringes of society? My sermons often encouraged people to make lunch dates with those least liked in their workplace. Our world contains much hurt, and if well-equipped, our members can carry Jesus' mission to the downtrodden.

Morphing to Disciplemaking

How does friendmaking morph into disciplemaking?

Someone once asked me, "When do I ask a non-believer if I can disciple them?" The answer is never. This is a stealth process.

Teaching people to share their hurts and doubts about spiritual matters is essential. Prayer is a bridge between a healthy friendship and a discipling relationship. We've trained people to present the wisdom of God, but joining wisdom to power generates effectiveness. The Greek words *sophia* ("wisdom") and *dunamis* ("power") reinforce each other. Jesus used the two when he linked the Spirit's power to the message, "But you will receive power when the Holy Spirit has come upon you, and you will be my witnesses in Jerusalem and in all Judea and Samaria, and to the end of the earth" (Acts 1:8, ESV).

We're not talking about prayer to accept Christ—at least not yet. It is prayer about something bothering an individual. Mutually shared stories, victories, and defeats pave the way for the kind of prayer that shifts toward ongoing conversations toward Christ. Prayer opportunities arise when a friend complains about a problem. If I've grown close enough to that person that they would accept it, I'll pray with them. Later, I'll ask them to pray for me about my needs. I may not yet be sure who they are praying to, but the act of a Christ-follower asking the pre-Christian for prayer opens new vistas.

Linking Story to Story

Getting to the "prayer point" is more accessible if everyday missionaries become adept at storytelling, preceded by story listening. The people we meet generally possess a poor picture of Christianity and the Church. Many have suffered pain at the hands of Christians, perhaps their parents or another family member. Depictions of Christians have poisoned many people via movies and other media. Church politics have caused much damage. Allowing people to air their stories freely opens a door for us to share ours.

Most of us have our own stories of family pain, Church-inflicted emotional damage, or questions about the Bible. Admitting these gives us credibility with those we are discipling toward Jesus. We also have stories of positive experiences countering the negative ones, or we wouldn't believe as we do. Sharing the mix brings reality to the discussion.

We live in a world that no longer believes in moral absolutes and universal truths. However, people still search for identity in a community. Friendship is significant to this need. Everyone responds well to whatever works for them in the here and now. They do not want to hear about pie in the sky. Most people hunger for a life-giving spirituality, but it must be personal, experiential, and pragmatic. Sharing real-life stories of personal doubt, faith, and spiritual victories opens doors to sharing spiritual reality in the everyday mission field.

I like to ask people, "Is there a God story in your life?" Another effective question is, "If there is a God, what do you think is your part in his story?" That question has initiated some deep discussions that have led to people moving toward Jesus. The question is powerful because after you listen—sometimes for days—to another person's perception of God, they will inevitably turn the question back to you. You earn the right to tell about your experience of God by listening to them describe theirs.

CHAPTER 14

AVOIDING POTHOLES

I had just sat down to eat my hot dog when the man sharing our table informed me that people, including him, were against religion. My wife and I were celebrating our 53rd wedding anniversary at a Ringo Starr concert in Los Angeles. We grabbed food at a concession outside the venue and soon found ourselves in an interesting conversation. I'm OK with crowds but shy with strangers, so talking with the guy was a relative miracle.

Overhearing Ruby and I converse about our life and ministry, the guy asked what I do for a job. I described my role in training Christ-followers to make disciples and plant churches. He bluntly informed me, "People are against religion, you know." Scrambling for a response, I told him of the tiny but growing interest in Jesus across Europe. He grew polite and asked about my travels there.

I somehow stumbled into telling him about a side trip my wife and I made to the beaches of Normandy. The mention of Normandy piqued his interest. A mini-friendship unfolded around our mutual interest in World War 2 and the Allied invasion of Hitler's Europe. We were a little late for the concert as he and I discussed books we had both read about D-Day. Our mutual interest turned what began as a hostile confrontation into a fun experience.

This budding friendship opened doors into this man's life. While we discussed the war and its aftermath, I brought the conversation to the post-war European disillusionment with God. I mentioned the spiritual vacuum many European friends had escaped when coming to Christ.

The man showed genuine interest, at which point his wife reminded us to get inside because we were missing part of the concert. I don't remember his name. We live far apart and will never meet again. The conversation lasted no more than 25 minutes, but in a short time, I was able to build a bridgehead into a life otherwise numb toward the gospel.

My point? Where argument fails, friendship wins. It is easy to share Jesus when we take the time to build a friendship around what we have in common before bringing up the faith we do not share. Now, if I can just get over my struggle with talking to strangers . . .

Respect the Good in the Surrounding Culture

My encounter at the concert would have ended much differently had I gotten defensive or aggressive. There often comes a point when you have to take a deep breath and look for something good in where that person is coming from (no matter how small) and then move toward common ground. The best example I can find of someone finding something commendable in a pagan culture is the apostle Paul during his brief sojourn in Athens (Acts 17).

Paul didn't make a lot of headway in Athens, but it was still progress. I like to think he functioned as a spiritual archaeologist, searching for hidden treasure, digging deeper where he sensed an opportunity. (We'll explore this concept further in a later chapter.)

Paul discovered and demonstrated respect for the theology of the people he wanted to reach. Sincere believers can damage their prospects by disrespecting the spiritual worldview of those they would evangelize. The "foreignness" of unfamiliar socio-religious groups and the "theology" of agnostics and atheists can become a barrier to effective disciplemaking.

Paul didn't trash Athenian theology. He built on it. He didn't judge or address their morality or their self-driven culture. He constructed inroads by identifying whatever value he found, linking their truth to a greater truth. Paul used the culture to reach the culture. And if you can equip people to do the same, you can raise a host of everyday missionaries.

Don't Impose Morality on Pre-Christians

Lutheran pastor turned Catholic priest Richard John Neuhaus wrote, "Politics is chiefly a function of culture; at the heart of culture is morality, and at the heart of morality is religion."[5] Apart from spiritual grounding, to change a culture's politics is a virtual impossibility (aside from martial law and rule at the barrel of a gun).

We live in a politically divided nation that has relegated Christianity to a step along the course of cultural and political evolution. The role of an everyday missionary is paramount in a culture that has forsaken its roots in Christianity for somewhat nefarious secularism. We won't accomplish much if we politicize the gospel or attack individuals for being a product of the world around them. We need to separate pre-Christians from our moral judgment, as righteousness comes from faith, not works.

I'm not sure about you, but I'm pretty good at judging others based on their vocabulary, tattoos, or sexual orientation. It is sobering to ponder how the body of Christ is collectively guilty of judging behaviors while proclaiming that justification comes by faith alone.

If we live what we believe, we will grow more effective at discipling people into Christ—moving them from where they are to where God would take them. To trust God rather than ourselves or our institutions to effect change requires confidence in the Holy Spirit to convict people of sin. We should never usurp his role.

The churches I led crafted a slogan to prevent us from playing Holy Spirit. We decided he was the policeman regarding behaviors, which was never our role. We expressed this in a slogan, "We promise to love you . . . as is!" Poor grammar but valuable sentiment. Those few words helped prevent us from judging outsiders and encouraged us to befriend them instead. Those words also kept us from trampling spiritual seedlings by imposing morality on new believers. And we found that people exposed to the Word and the Spirit experienced sanctification leading to holy lives.

Remember, the faith walk began with God asking one man to take a long walk. On his journey, he lied, committed adultery, and abandoned one son in favor of the other. He was justified by faith, and thank God, the principle stands as firm today as it did when Abram left Mesopotamia. Our problem is in remembering that standard when we encounter someone living in a less-than-godly manner.

Overt disapproval of behaviors often undermines the possibility of relationships. No one was ever judged into the Kingdom of God—especially if people in our camp act a lot like those we judge. The news media is replete with moral failures among Christian leaders. In Romans 2, Paul assaults religious people for attacking those around us while living as hypocrites. We should pay attention to his sentiments.

After setting out several reasons for disfellowshipping a believer, Paul wrote, "For what have I to do with judging outsiders? Is it not those inside the church whom you are to judge?" (1 Corinthians 5:12, ESV). There's a place for judgment, and it begins in the House of God. It doesn't extend to people who don't yet know Christ. Nor does it apply to people who are still learning to walk with him.

Don't Make Enemies

Churches sadden me with their near mindless alignment with the political right or left. It's easy to find ourselves opposing righteousness in those we should befriend.

Several decades ago, Francis Schaeffer, a pastor and Christian philosopher taught that we should be "co-belligerents" with either the political right or left whenever they champion a righteous position. Adopting a political party line can only undermine the mission of the Church.

The decision to wear a mask or not is hardly a hill upon which to die—and certainly not worth separating your church from the surrounding society. Conversely, the civil rights movement was and is a cause worthy of Christ-followers who believe Jesus came to "set at liberty those who are oppressed" (Luke 4:18, ESV). Oppression supersedes party politics, as does a righteous response to it.

The temptation to align with one political group or a specific leader in totality is dangerous. It inevitably makes enemies of those doing the same thing on the opposite side of the fence. One of my friends is a gay man who constantly tries to pigeonhole me alongside the political right. I can hold God's Word above the chaos by refusing to blindly adopt any party line. That is slowly opening the mind of my extremely political friend.

Aside from politics, other areas of enmity are music, art, and clothing styles. I don't approve of a lot I see around me, but I dare not allow my disapproval to morph into antagonism toward those who embrace these things.

Music and art often speak prophetically to agony and unrighteousness. The protest songs of the 1960s and 1970s (which I continually play) did this in ways I approve of. I struggle with hip-hop and rap music because of language and other issues. Becoming better acquainted with a couple of artists in person and through watching TV interviews gave me an appreciation for what they try to communicate. Appreciation of a message doesn't mean I embrace an artist or a musician without examining their output. It does require me to withhold the judgment that would make an enemy where there is none.

Art and music represent forces you must understand, at least if you expect to equip your people to effectively evangelize the world they face daily. Equipping our members to relate to others through cultural means will help them reach beyond intellectual arguments to emotions that can change thinking.

When I was younger, the surrounding culture generally viewed the Bible as the Word of God, though people may have ignored its claims. That has changed. There is now little respect for the Bible. However, people still search for something that works for them. We can't show them how Jesus works in our lives unless we argue against those cultural elements crying out for the righteousness we espouse.

Understanding "Truth" in a Post-Christian Era

We must look beyond dogma. Most people aren't looking for universal truth, though some may "pray to the universe." We need to lead friends into truth that works for them and then help them deduce the universal from the local as they delve into the Scriptures.

We must realize that when somebody attacks the Church or asks why God would allow evil, they may reflect on personal experiences. Our people will hear the distress in the form of questions or slander. Getting into the emotion behind a discussion opens spiritual doors.

We must understand that identity, truth, and community are interconnected. At some level, all of us gather identity from our relationships. We display our social attachments in our choices of clothing, jewelry, and body markings. Our identity is also reflected in political alignments. Finding identity in a group shows up in everything from street gangs to private membership at a golf or tennis club. Group approval is central to church experience.

Social identity expresses itself in the feelings of self-worth people gain from being accepted into a cadre of others, whether formal or informal. Group identification can explain the horrors of bullying and racism. The "truths" espoused by the group become an accepted reality to its members. This makes it crucial for us to equip our members to build friendships in outside social groups while freely welcoming their members into our own. Jesus taught us to remain in the household of a person of peace. When an everyday missionary gains entry to a friend's cultural group, that person becomes more effective.

Love Even Your Enemies

Paul described religious Pharisees and early Christian legalists as enemies of the cross. His observation is as accurate today as when he penned it. Add to the list those people who see the Church as an impediment to social progress. We have natural enemies, whether we choose them or not.

Here's the deal: Jesus died for your enemies when he died for you and me. We need to remind our people that he wasn't kidding when he called us to love our enemies and that we are to pray for those who despitefully use us. As a pastor, I needed this reminder whenever dealing with a city building department or when our landlords joined a lawsuit to keep us from building on the property they leased to us.

Jesus calls us to love those who would attack us. Some of our most extraordinary church planting results came via the radical disciple-making of a man who came to church to beat up the pastor (me) but met love before he could do the deed. One of the man's disciples accounts for close to 15% of the churches planted in the Hope Chapel movement.

I want to end this chapter by stressing friendship evangelism as a process of disciplemaking, where the line between unbelief and belief gets blurred. We have too often drawn lines to decide who's in and who's out. We need to begin to think of a disciplemaking continuum, perhaps looking at where this person is on a scale of 1 to 100. Measuring the grayscale differs from pressing people to pray a little prayer that puts them across the goal line when we stamp their forehead as an authentic Christ-follower. We can embrace people with whom Jesus is not yet finished, bring them into our community, and hopefully join with theirs. However, it is paramount that ours is a community practicing love, acceptance, and forgiveness—otherwise everyone loses.

CHAPTER 15

CREATING A FRAMEWORK FOR EVERYDAY MISSIONS

E arly American graveyards bristle with headstones topped with symbols of a skull and crossbones. These macabre symbols signify death, the ultimate destroyer. The headstones also bear epitaphs describing the life of the person buried below. One thought-provoking epitaph reads, "I told you I was sick!"

What five or six words best describe your church? Are you sick or healthy? How do you know? No one wants to say, "I'm a member of a sick church." The apostle Paul gave us some pointers toward church health in the fourth chapter of Ephesians. To the degree that leaders equip members for ministry, the congregation is healthy. Wherever this is lacking, the leader needs a dose of medicine from the Holy Spirit.

A Hospital Church Is an Equipping Church

A healthy church is a "hospital church." The signs are simple: this church is well-doctored by its leaders. Every incoming patient eventually finds a place on the healing team. As they grow, they build up the church by ministering to each other and evangelizing their friends and neighbors. Learning to minister to "one another" helps equip our members to minister to the neighbors. Our teaching, strategy, and systems must focus on equipping members for ministry in intentional, relational, and consistent ways.

Everyone comes to the Lord very sick with sin. Only those who grow interested in healing others gain full health. They won't achieve perfection but will approach spiritual maturity.

I love the term *practicing medicine*. How often has your doctor prescribed medicine in *hopes* that it will work for you? A couple of weeks ago, my doctor gave me a new medicine. Medical journals suggested positive results *apart from* the specific purpose for which it was created. He wanted me to see whether it would help my particular problem (it did). In other words, he tested the medicine on me to see whether it helped me and whether it would help others. He was "practicing" medicine.

Churches that allow and encourage Christians to test their ministry abilities are healthy. Churches where Christians freely attempt to do the work of God are healthy. Those that do not, are not.

Healthy Christians are those growing toward maturity in knowledge and ministry skills. They hold the truth in love. The Bible is the "medical" handbook. Members of a healthy church use it, rather than argue about it.

Members of a healthy church can identify their unique calling from God. To fully participate, our members need to understand their spiritual gifts. They also need growing faith to realize that they only have to offer the prayers and never need to answer them. We often have not because we ask not from him who can do "far more than we could ever ask for or imagine" (Ephesians 3:20, NIrV). Such confidence releases them to "practice Holy Spirit medicine." A healthy church is a local display of the body of Christ. This "hospital church" touches the world as its members minister according to the spiritual gifts God invested in each person.

I recently met Chloe, who is a gifted 20-year-old evangelist. Bubbly and excitable, she is aware of her gifting and has used it to plant a microchurch in a park. She gathered a few friends, bought four pizzas, and invaded a Southern California fishing pier. While giving away pizza slices to homeless people, she invites them to church in the nearby park. Linking individual prayer to the Scriptures has produced miraculous life changes in these people. Not everyone is an evangelist, but every member needs to learn to trigger their unique gifts and calling. It is our job to help them do that.

A Disciplemaking Continuum

So how does this progression from patient to healer work? We call the process a disciplemaking continuum. A disciplemaking continuum is a pathway from unbelief to mature function in the body of Christ. Every church has one—for example, weekend teaching plus small group interaction as preparation for entering the everyday mission field.

A Disciplemaking Continuum

A disciplemaking continuum is the combined efforts of a church to disciple its members at every level and in every ministry. These efforts vary in their outcomes. Some leaders equip others with knowledge for knowledge's sake. Others focus on holy living or sanctification. Paul seemed to include knowledge and sanctification when he challenged us to equip members for ministry. I'm describing his desired outcome as spiritual healers and everyday missionaries.

Lead Pastors as Disciplemakers, or Not?

The major obstacle to equipping every member as an everyday missionary might be the person reading this book—the lead pastor. Lead pastors lead and drive their congregation's disciplemaking continuum. Every pastor wants to maximize effectiveness. Most can't describe a straightforward pathway from the front door to the mission field. Whatever they built, many remain somewhat aloof to the process—they design it then delegate it to others.

The equipping pathway begins with disciplemaking as a significant priority in your job description. How can you expect others to do what you don't? You should be able to name your three closest disciples without much thought. If you can't do this, you must re-read Jesus' words in Matthew 28.

Is disciplemaking a private project between you and a few friends? Is disciplemaking integral to your church family? Is disciplemaking the central organizing principle or an add-on to your church's primary purpose and function? Are you building a hospital church?

These are essential questions we need to ask ourselves over a ministry tenure. Why? Because it's easy to start well and finish poorly. This is not uncommon for those pastors who got into ministry by making disciples. They later back off as they become overwhelmed with managing a congregation.

Disciplemaking is central to any hope of multiplying the Church. Disciples who make disciples are key to any hope of shaping the culture by mobilizing everyday missionaries. Yet many pastors say they are too busy to do the third-most-important thing Jesus commanded after loving God and loving our neighbors.

CHAPTER 16

IS YOUR CONTINUUM EFFECTIVE?

So, let's talk about *your* disciplemaking continuum. Is there a clear path, or do you present a scattered hodgepodge of disassociated training venues you call discipleship? Do your small groups, home groups, or cell groups meet consistently or in stuttered spurts? Are they ongoing enough to call them microchurches within the circle of your congregation (as opposed to those sent out to minister to other people groups)?

Scattered

Many pastors can't describe a clear path to maturity. "Well, you take this class, then join this group, and also we provide a seminar, etc." There is no direct and easily identifiable continuum. The process is scattered. When pastors cannot describe a direct pathway to maturity, their people are just as confused.

Stuttered

Many disciplemaking continuums struggle because they stutter. Stuttering describes the start-and-stop nature of many home groups or microchurches within the congregation.

Many, if not most, congregations host stuttered groups at the core of their disciplemaking continuums. Groups gather for eight weeks, followed by a four-week break. After the hiatus, they regroup, meeting with different people and examining a different curriculum. Some meet for eight or nine months. Continuity gets interrupted by a summer break. There's little opportunity for those people to fall in love with one another.

I spoke with a California pastor who complained because many of his best leaders were moving out of state. They moved because of high real-estate costs or disapproval of our political system. He recently admonished the congregation to ask God whether he *is calling* them to California. Or does he want them to move to another state? This challenge generated some positive dialogue, but the pastor was still dissatisfied. He acknowledged that the church members didn't remain in community with each other long enough to bond with one another—that bonding would contribute to staying power. People who deeply love one another think twice before moving apart.

Three Legs Under a Disciplemaking Continuum

We built a disciplemaking continuum around just three Scriptures. The package would ultimately influence everything taught from the pulpit.

A Statement of Purpose

In Ephesians 4, we discover that Jesus' *purpose* for gifts is to equip ordinary people to build the Church as healthy members and everyday missionaries.

Deploying Unique Masterpieces

Paul describes those saved by grace as "God's handiwork. We are created in Christ Jesus to do good works, which God prepared in advance for us to do" (Ephesians 2:10, NIV). There is little room for spectators in this scenario. Our job as equippers is to find ways to deploy God's handiwork in meaningful daily ministry. A Holy Spirit-empowered culture produces Spirit-led people using their gifts in the world.

Describing Function and Form

The third Scripture undergirding our ministry came from the Church's earliest history. The book of Acts communicates much about the *function* of what we call the Church. Acts 2 presents an interesting problem. The Church grew from 120 to 3,000 believers in a single day. Meeting in small homes would require 300-plus new converts to serve as house-church leaders on the day after Pentecost. These people met in the temple courts, where the apostles taught, and in homes, where there weren't enough apostles to cover the bases.

The result was that the Church indulged in the apostle's teaching, fellowship, prayer, eating, giving, praising God, and getting along with the neighbors. They probably did the neighbor thing better than many of us today. Can you name the people living in the three houses on either side of yours?

The teaching element set us on a path toward a workable model or *form* for our life together. Because form follows function, we developed very simple structures around these Scriptures.

Assuming these neophytes oversaw the apostle's teaching in homes, we must also assume that they *reflected* whatever the apostles taught in public spaces. As a maturing church plant, we decided that we could arm our lawyers, engineers, hippies, and truck drivers to lead small groups or microchurches. Microchurch leaders asked meaningful questions to help our members reflect on whatever the Holy Spirit spoke to their hearts in public meetings.

This approach linked the power of the pulpit (apostles' teaching) to everyday missionaries (favor with neighbors while God added to his Church). For us, the middle ground between the pulpit and the gospel in shoe leather was the ministry going on in our small groups. These functioned as microchurches *inside* our congregation. Asking our people to do more than assess a message intellectually, we invited them to evaluate and apply God's revelation to their lives and immediate futures.

CHAPTER 17

A MEETING TEMPLATE

We joined the Sunday services to the microchurch meetings by incorporating four questions designed to equip our people for ministry. After listening to a weekend Bible teaching, small groups would come together to discuss what they heard—linking the pulpit to the pew, so to speak. If people weren't able to hear the weekend teaching, we asked them to share only after hearing responses from the rest of the group. (This became easier when we were able to post our weekend teaching on the internet.) These small churches grew by ministering to one another and by becoming familiar with talking about God in non-religious ways. Finally, they would experience the power of the Spirit through answered prayer, which bolstered their courage when interacting with acquaintances outside the congregation.

A Question of Hearing

The first question was: "What did the Spirit speak to you while you listened to a Bible teaching on the weekend?" We assumed that the Spirit may have used the speaker's words to speak directly to the listener's heart. We discovered that even when a person daydreamed in church, the Spirit was always speaking, and that person would come away with a personal message. The overriding goal was to teach our people to be open to hearing God's still, small voice.

A Question of Obeying

The second question was: "What will you do because of what the Spirit revealed to you?" At this point, people move from hearing God to doing what he says.

When your members declare a course of action to their friends, they will likely follow through. They may have decided to reach out to a person in the workplace, to swear off pornography, or to begin tithing. Whatever the issue, a public declaration engrains a measure of accountability to the decision.

A Question of Serving

The third question was: "How can we help or pray with (or for) you?" The answers sometimes awakened dormant spiritual gifts in other group members. Serving one another helped folks appreciate the unique "masterpiece" God created in them when they met Christ.

A spiritual-gifts profile is a handy tool, but getting people involved in serving one another is more powerful. Compassion is a great discovery-driver relating to spiritual gifts. People discover their gifts as they begin to walk in them.

Some answers to group prayer were spectacular. All of them built faith in our members. We'd pray one week and find ourselves hearing God stories while sharing food as we opened the meetings in the following weeks. Stories of God working through our members may have been called "testimony time" in an earlier era.

A Question of Telling

The question I wish we had added to our profile is: "Who else needs to know what you've told us?" That question may have brought healing to families as a person revealed new insight into their attitudes or behaviors. Answering the question would have helped an everyday missionary frame whatever they hoped to say to their friend. The idea would be to take skills learned—and interaction with the Spirit and the group—into their daily interactions with others.

Linking Pulpit to Pew	
Hearing	What did the Spirit speak to you?
Obeying	What will you do because of what the Spirit spoke?
Serving	How can we help you or pray with you?
Telling	Who else should know about this?

A Typical Meeting

Pastors often ask about a schedule or timetable for a small-group meeting. I hesitate to provide one, as that can turn an organic experience into a program. But here goes . . .

We began with food, as people tend to open up when eating together. That was also a time for members to share whatever they had experienced with God or how they supported each other as a result of the previous meetings. The food also allowed someone who worked late to show up later, rather than miss the meeting to catch dinner.

After hanging out around snacks, the leader asked each individual for two or three words they remembered from the weekend teaching. The object was to take the memory out of the mental file cabinet and put it on the table. After this, each member would answer the four questions. We'd go around the circle, with each person sharing their answers and experiences. However, sometimes we would break from the format to concentrate on the needs of a person who had been moved by their interaction with the Spirit. Getting through the questions or having each person speak was not as important as experiencing life-changing ministry.

The meeting ended with each person praying about something they heard another say during our time together. We discouraged "prayer requests," as we wanted to stick to issues important enough to naturally surface during the gathering.

CHAPTER 18

A CULTURE OF COMMUNICATION

These simple meetings superseded much pastoral counseling and several church programs, releasing time and money that we directed toward planting churches. But the kicker was evangelism. We had built a "culture of communication." As our members grew comfortable speaking of their interactions with the Spirit and the spoken word, they became less fearful of discussing spiritual matters. This spilled over into their daily lives.

As these groups grew into families, our people grew more open with each other. Shy people learned to share feelings and insights in a safe environment. The relationships born in small groups built courage into our members. The environment generated planned spontaneity, where conversations flowed along the lines of shared needs and mutual insights.

As people learned to communicate transparently with one another, those conversations prepared them to communicate with people outside our church. In Hawaii, we saw entire families come to Christ because one member had found Jesus through someone in our church. Sharing stories, doubts, and prayers in the microchurch set people up to do the same with folks outside the church.

Perhaps the most significant bonus to church this way came as church multiplication. We challenged leaders to train apprentices and then "hive off" to form a new group. Whenever someone did this three times, I would ask them to pray about planting a church away from ours. Most did not, but those who did touched a broader world. Training for a church plant required much more preparation than would fit on these pages. But this simple framework produced churches while equipping members as everyday missionaries.

Another thing I would do differently if I were leading a congregation today is plant microchurches outside our congregation as a startup plan. This approach would replace the mid-size plants we normally launched. We invested tremendous money and sent large groups to plant churches. Today, in light of our more anti-Church culture and high real-estate costs, I would approach church planting from a micro perspective. This approach would let the new church grow without regard for raising enough money to meet costly budgets. It would eliminate the temptation for leaders to build around transfer growth. And it would allow us to multiply more often.

Examining Your Efforts

The best thing about structuring as we did is that it was simple, effective, and scalable. If whatever we did wouldn't pass this basic test, we considered modifying or dropping it.

Simple

We built a model so simple that anyone could operate it after having experienced it. Techniques are better caught than taught, so skill was always passed along by a disciple serving alongside a mentor. Pilots and doctors attend college to gain knowledge, but on-the-job training provides the necessary skills to do their jobs. Our model centered on on-the-job training, with the book knowledge built into ongoing leadership development as we studied together. Normally around 15% of our leaders were reading books in concert then discussing them in small clusters. We used the four questions from the microchurch meetings in our reading collectives.

Effective

For us, the norm was 50–60% involvement in our disciplemaking continuum. Over several decades, consistently training so many people in community produced thousands of effective everyday missionaries and hundreds of church planters. We succeeded in activating spiritual gifts by blending the weekend meetings with small-group experiences. Doing so tied the Word to the Spirit in the minds and hearts of individuals. It also got people comfortable with speaking about God. Serving one another inside the family helped raise alertness to spiritual gifts, which we encouraged for service outside the circle of our congregations.

Scalable

Because our reflection model was our church's organizing principle, we replicated it (as *distinct* from duplicating it) at four levels: 1) it was our primary model for microchurches within the circle of our congregation; 2) it became our tool for leadership training groups; 3) it could work with two or three friends in the marketplace; and 4) we could train people in other countries to utilize it. We discovered a great advantage to our model in poverty-ridden cultures that could not afford the various curriculums used by many Western churches.

Throw Yourself into This

Have you noticed the *movement* in Paul's words to his disciple Timothy? "So, my son, throw yourself into this work for Christ. Pass on what you heard from me . . . to reliable leaders who are competent to teach others" (2 Timothy 2:1-2, MSG).

First, Paul tells Timothy to "throw" himself into "this work for Christ." What work? Disciplemaking. Paul instructs Timothy to take what he has learned from Paul and pass it along to reliable people capable of teaching others.

I don't know about you, but I count five levels of disciples in that passage: 1) Paul (a protégé of Barnabas); 2) Timothy; 3) reliable leaders; 4) other competent teachers; and 5) those who would learn from these teachers. (By the way, don't let the word *teachers* throw you off; Paul is talking about everyday people teaching what they know to other people.)

An effective disciplemaking continuum is not a program to bolt onto a congregation. It is a church built around a simple, effective, scalable disciplemaking model. It links the pulpit to the streets outside the church through a process where members integrate their lives with the message they hear. And it requires a lead pastor to "throw" himself into the process. Whenever I've observed a lead pastor personally involved in a disciplemaking continuum, I've seen evangelism working in the marketplace. And there is usually the ability to multiply the church. Throw yourself into this, and you'll bless a lot of people.

Don't Ignore the Heromaking Element

This chapter wouldn't be complete if we didn't link whatever goes on in the microchurches and marketplace back to the pulpit.

Your church culture combines many things, but the basics are values, narratives, and behaviors. You teach your values. Some people live them better than others. Putting their exploits on display in your weekend teaching makes heroes of these people. Their narratives spark similar behaviors in others. If you haven't already read it, you may want to look at Dave Ferguson and Warren Bird's book, *Heromaker: Five Essential Practices for Leaders to Multiply Leaders.*[6] Though not specifically directed toward equipping everyday missionaries, their book will strengthen you as you equip others to share faith.

Delving into redundancy, I want to reinforce that a culture of disciplemaking is the structure to support everyday missionaries. You can lead your church as a disciplemaking continuum beginning with your values, moving through your forms or structures, and ending by exalting those values. Doing so, you will find that evangelism in a post-Christian era is more than doable; it's natural.

CHAPTER 19

QUESTIONS TO ASK, STORIES TO TELL

Arming your members with a few simple questions is helpful. And it's essential to coach people about the kinds of stories their friends can easily relate to.

Nonbelievers have spiritual opinions and like to talk about them, particularly relating to personal experiences. The tricky part is equipping our members not to argue but to engage. The goal is to discover where others are in their journey and to be prepared to share things with them.

Questions to Ask

Here are a few questions to open doors to spiritual conversations:

- Have you ever had what you might call a spiritual experience? If you did, how did it feel?
- Assuming there is a God, how would you describe him?
- What do you think about prayer? How does it work in your life?

The danger in such questions is the responses others give. It's important to never fall prey to the temptation to offer corrections to strange answers, which can lead to arguments.

The Best Stories

I've always felt that an individual should reserve their conversion story for late in the process of disciplemaking. It fits only after building a solid relationship with someone who displays an open heart. Otherwise, it can feel like sales pressure. Save it for those who have grown interested in Jesus.

It's appealing to tell another person, "This is how I came to Christ, and here's the difference he made in my life." The assumption is that this is how they will come to faith. We need to remember that they will not follow the same path we did. No two people are alike.

Concurrently, people are saved by the blood of the Lamb and the word of their (and our) testimony (Revelation 12:11). Our testimony of Christ is of paramount importance, but we must discern whatever part of our story is appropriate at a particular moment. Few pre-Christians are interested in conversion stories. They are, however, intrigued by stories relating to their own story.

A parallel story from a Christ-follower is meaningful when someone expresses anger over church hurt. Knowing that a believer has experienced a wrong from another Christian opens a door to empathy from the pre-Christian. When they tell of an unusual spiritual experience or an unanswerable question, they will welcome such experiences and questions in the life of a believer. It is also necessary to coach people toward freely comingling a parable or miracle story from the New Testament whenever appropriate. Passing along a favorite psalm is an excellent way to introduce a pre-believer to the Bible. Hearing and sharing stories partnered with relevant Scripture hopefully leads to mutual prayers and discussion over how God answers them.

When pre-Christian friends share a meaningful experience, a believer might respond with, "You know that triggers a thought" or

"There's a story in the Bible that is somewhat parallel to yours." Sharing stories is productive in a post-Christian culture. When personal and friendly, storytelling flies beneath the radar of cynicism and political attack.

So, as we're telling our stories, it's effective to introduce stories of change that God has worked in us or in other people's lives. Again, we're hailing the miraculous. I teach people to ask themselves, "What has God done to answer my prayers?" and "How has God changed a mutual friend from a life of degradation or, perhaps, alcoholism to a life of health and healing?" I encourage members to refrain from drawing religious conclusions from their stories. Their friends will draw their own spiritual inferences from the shared stories. It's best to present the story and then go quiet. If the individual wants to know more, they will ask.

The Right Time for the Conversion Story

When is it time to bring the conversion story into the relationship? A personal conversion story is appropriate to share with someone who appears to believe in their heart but hasn't yet fully come to grips with belief on an intellectual level. The never-never land between emotional and intellectual belief requires patience on the part of the missionary. Paul described the gospel as a stumbling block, foolishness and weakness to outsiders. Yet he called it the power and wisdom of God to believers (1 Corinthians 1:22-25). A friend in this valley of understanding between foolishness and wisdom might need a helpful nudge. This is the time to look for an opportunity to pray a conversion prayer, which might happen in a church service or in the quiet of a home. The goal of the everyday missionary is to bring a friend to a point of belief and understanding. The Spirit will do the rest.

CHAPTER 20

DISCOVERING A PERSONAL MISSION FIELD

One of my friends just moved from San Diego to Hilo, Hawaii, where he's planting a church. Beginning as a microchurch, it will multiply at that level or outgrow the "micro" and then multiply. Either way, it will act as a hub for church multiplication.

The guy is clever; he began by looking for persons of peace before announcing anything. A building contractor who surfs and produces expensive wood art, Billy makes friends easily. His goal is to gain friendships with different people groups in a relatively small town. Seeking new friends is an obvious step when planting a church. We must equip our members to do this where they live *now* if we hope to take the gospel outside the comfort of our congregation to a hurting and often hostile world.

While checking out the area before he moved, Billy connected with the "king" of a surf spot near his soon-to-be home. Jumping into the water as a tourist or a newbie can be off-putting to locals, if not dangerous to you. Locals don't take kindly to outsiders—especially outsiders from the mainland, as many locals resent mainlanders for moving to Hawaii and changing its landscape (along with its real estate prices). So, Billy waited in the parking lot to speak with the guy who dominated the surf session. He approached this Hawaiian man with an apology for "what people who look like me have done to people who look like you." His humility touched a live nerve.

The guy was taken aback by the request for forgiveness and immediately opened up to his new friend. Billy then asked permission to surf "at your spot." His humble approach unlocked the door to further conversation, and the man launched into an abbreviated version of his life and troubles at home. At that point, Billy asked if he could pray with him (all this in an initial conversation—I told you he is gregarious). Billy's new friend agreed, with tears in his eyes. After the prayer, he told Billy, "You should start a church or something."

Billy can describe similar experiences at a hole-in-the-wall coffee shop and at a community college, where he joined an "open Saturday" group in which the public gets to use the school's woodshop. He is reaching his kinds of people in their social context. Because Billy is so friendly and outgoing, he compresses weeks and months of evangelistic processes into hours and minutes. His life is an excellent example, though hardly a template. He is a "spiritual archaeologist," and I've learned to use stories like Billy's to inspire and equip others.

Spiritual Archaeologists

An archaeologist searches for hidden treasure. Theirs is seldom a random search. They follow a suspected trail of evidence toward a prize. Occasionally they will stumble onto something unexpected, but mostly they know where they will find the good stuff.

A spiritual archaeologist is someone equipped to pursue similar leads, digging where they sense opportunity. Sharing faith with an unbeliever is much like an archaeologist gently removing soil from a buried object of great value—sometimes with a shovel, but often with a fine brush. Some people won't be ready to receive the gospel, but the bigger issue is that our people are simply unaware of their place in God's great story. Planting missionary thoughts in their minds is huge when equipping Church members as everyday missionaries.

We can equip our people for spiritual archaeology by helping them assess their mission field and the best steps into the lives of others. This process includes asking where they should take their good news and discerning what the Spirit is doing in the life of another person.

An important example is Jesus' interchange with the demonized man in Gerasenes (Mark 5). After being set free from Satan's grip, the man begged to travel with Jesus. Jesus refused the request while extending a greater purpose for the man's life. Jesus instructed the man to return home and tell of what the master had done for him. The word that translates "home" in our English Bibles is *oikon* or *oikos*, which generally speaks of an extended household, including friends and even employees. Surrounded by millions, each church member lives in such a household. Every one of us has a private village. This circle is where we can most effectively share what Jesus has done for us and for others.

The Church growth movement taught us to construct "fishing ponds" by staging events where people could invite their friends. These artificial constructs are expensive, can degenerate into shallow outcomes, and often rob time from disciplemaking. While producing converts, they make more spectators than everyday missionaries. The approach overlooks the reality that each of us lives in an organic fishing pool. These include friends, coworkers, and neighbors. Special interest groups may be the most fruitful of the *oikos* surrounding everyone you know. It's our job to heighten awareness of the missionary call on our members to their *oikos*.

The follow-me-as-I-follow-Christ dynamic is a straightforward path to evangelism in any culture, especially one that sidelines the Church. I've always tried to get our people to visualize their personal Jerusalem as they relate to Acts 1:8, "But you will receive power when the Holy Spirit has come upon you, and you will be my witnesses in Jerusalem and in all Judea and Samaria, and to the end of the earth" (ESV). Whenever teaching from Acts 2, I press church members to reach out to their immediate neighbors and workmates.

The goal is to inspire everyday missionaries as they ask themselves the following questions:

Who Are My Kind of People?

The Bible gives us direction as we answer this question. The first place Barnabas and Saul went to from Antioch was Cyprus, Barnabas' home culture. He was a Jew who grew up in a Gentile community. He was part of an *oikos* network of friends and family members on the island. Later, we find the pair in Antioch of Pisidia, near Tarsus. We don't know much about Paul's life in Tarsus, but we can safely assume that he understood his kind of people as well.

I'm a wannabe surfer and a car nut. I ate lunch with a circle of African American friends for four years of high school. Surfers, car guys, and African Americans are easy for me to engage. My first real job was in a company owned and populated mainly by Asian Americans. Later, I spent a lot of time in Asia. Though I'm a white, middle-class, Christ-follower, these are also my kinds of people. My private culture attracts me to people whose experiences are similar to mine.

So as an equipper, I constantly ask church members, "Who are your kind of people?" "What inbuilt pathways do you have for spreading your good news?"

Jesus taught us to look for persons of peace in a new community. As a pastor, I always remained aware of persons of peace who were members of our church community. These folks were comfortable in our racially diverse, though thoroughly middle-class, congregation while deeply involved in people groups quite different from us. They may have been into martial arts (one of my friends planted a strong microchurch in a mixed martial arts studio), the medical community, surfers, community activists, etc. They may have been racially different from the main body of our church. Their membership in our congregation provided a pathway to communicate the gospel in a community separate from ours.

Who Is Reachable?

Paul and Barnabas primarily began ministry by proclaiming the gospel in synagogues. They would reap a few interested people—usually a mix of Jewish people and God-fearing Gentiles. They discipled their new followers, leaving a small community of believers in their wake as they moved to the next assignment.

So again, I want the people I equip to ask, "Who do I know that is hungry for God?" "Who is into an expression of mysticism or New Age spirituality?" "Which of my friends wants to argue about religion?" (because arguing often reflects unfulfilled spiritual hunger).

Social media presents insights into the lives of friends and workmates. Keeping alert to those posting religious material is one way to discover spiritual interest. The big question is, "Who in my *oikos* displays spiritual hunger, and how can I engage them on that level?"

Where Is God Already at Work?

Philip and Peter experienced Holy Spirit revelation toward evangelism; we should never overlook it. It took a word from the Lord to link Philip to the Ethiopian reading Scripture in his chariot. Peter needed a repeated vision to get to the house of the Roman officer. In both cases, these everyday missionaries followed the work of the Spirit into a person's heart, which spread to others through that individual.

I vividly remember an occasion when that still, small voice led me to speak with a man sitting in a street alcove awaiting the annual Rose Parade in Pasadena. The Spirit nudged me when I noticed a pair of jeans and booted feet protruding from an alcove in a storefront. I didn't know whether the person was male or female. But it seemed like the Lord was leading me to speak with them.

When I followed the lead, I met immediate resistance. The person wearing the boots was a young man mulling over his last few hours of freedom before entering the army. Because I felt God led me to him, I persevered past his opposition. A couple of hours later, he came to Christ (these were the days of street evangelism involving gospel literature). The kicker came when the youth leaders (now pastors) from my boyhood in Oregon showed up across the street from where my new friend and I watched the parade. Out of a crowd numbering more than a million people, I introduced this young man to these church leaders now living in his town (a thousand miles from where I had known them). I never connected with him again, but a few years later, those pastors told me he had returned from the army and was serving as a leader in their church.

Listening to God's voice is learned behavior. We can equip our people for sensitivity to the Holy Spirit that might lead to a prayer encounter between them and a person ready to hear the good news.

Where Is There Pain?

The New Testament story is replete with healings, demonic deliverance, etc. The early saints had extreme confidence in God answering prayer. They leaned into pain as a tool for inviting people to worship the Messiah.

Finding an opportunity to pray with people over personal problems opens doors. Along with physical distress, your people encounter everything from racism to church hurt to divorce. These are signals of need in a person's life.

Teach your people to make friends with hurting people. Trailheads can appear as depression, extreme anxiety, drug abuse, broken homes, and self-harm.

One of my friends resigned from our staff to "become the pastor" of a local company where a madman had killed five people with a gun. My friend initially met with gossip, describing him as a religious nut. However, he eventually led several co-workers to Christ and launched a string of successful microchurches that meet in the downtown Honolulu business district.

When we started churches in Hermosa Beach and Kaneohe, we ran ads explicitly targeting people with aching memories of shattered families or toxic churches. The results required intense disciplemaking, but they paid off. Pain is a pathway for the gospel.

Who Did God Put in My Path?

Upon moving to San Diego, my wife and I received two hand-written letters from a neighboring Jehovah's Witness woman. She asked questions about our feelings toward the world and its chaos. In her letters, she invited us to share coffee and discuss what the Bible says about turmoil in the last days. We never responded to her invitation, but we did appreciate her effort. She viewed us, her new neighbors, as people God put in her path.

Unlike her somewhat introverted husband, my wife freely engages with restaurant servers, hairdressers, and clerks where she shops.

During a period when she tutored struggling students in a public school, she prayed to meet their families outside of the campus. One afternoon while heading to a shopping mall, she bumped into the single mother of a boy she tutored. The lady had five kids in tow as she crossed a parking lot to her apartment. That short conversation instigated a friendship, and her entire family came to Christ and ended up living with a family in our congregation.

We've built a strong relationship with the realtor who helped us purchase our house. A lapsed Catholic, he now nearly *demands* that we pray together whenever we meet him for lunch. The list goes on. It's crucial that our members look for those whom God put in their lives as their personal mission field.

CHAPTER 21

BUILDING COMMUNITIES OUTSIDE THE BOX

When Paul and Silas met with Lydia and her crew near a river in Philippi, they touched a circle of Godfearers apart from any synagogue. Add the Philippian jailer to the mix, and they left behind a microchurch that served as the seed for something larger. We need to be open to similar activities on the fringes of our churches (while resisting the temptation to attach them to our congregation). These are often best coached to grow into something independent of us.

This brings to mind one such opportunity in my life that had both rewarding and hard lessons.

Opportunity Taken

A mother-daughter team belonged to one of our in-house microchurches. That group lost the apartment where they had been meeting, and they had nowhere to go. These two gracious ladies offered their home as a meeting place. Sadly, the microchurch leaders rebuffed their offer for reasons I won't describe here. Meanwhile, I was discipling a young man who was anxious to learn leadership and was looking for a meeting place in that particular community. The following week, my young disciple, one member of the original group, and my wife and I met at the home of that mother and daughter.

We arrived to find the husband/father, Hale, in the living room drinking beer and watching a Lakers game. Our tiny, intimidated crew scurried into the kitchen.

Hale had approved the use of the living room for our gathering, so I decided to watch the ballgame with him while the rest of our group met in the kitchen. At the end of the evening, we explained that we liked to wrap things up with a song, and we asked him to accompany us on his guitar. The kitchen crew joined us as he strummed along to our poor chorus. We then asked if he would play again as we sang the following week. He showed up at our next meeting sober and ready to display his musical ability. After several months of participation, he decided to follow Jesus.

Two important things happened in the aftermath. His adult sons and their families often stopped by the parents' house for snacks on their way home from softball games. Hanging out in the kitchen, they overheard their dad talk about his new alcohol-free life in Christ. After several months of this, they decided to follow their dad on his walk with Jesus. Both sons are now leaders in churches we planted.

Opportunity Missed

The other significant result was an evening when my new friend Hale left our group, guitar in hand, to minister to the crowd gathered at the home of a neighbor who had recently died. A few moments later, we heard worship songs coming from the despairing family.

I said this situation was both rewarding and hard. It was rewarding because an extended family came to Christ and became leaders in our churches—it was hard because I realized we had missed an opportunity to pursue Hale's and his family's expanded *oikos* in their neighborhood.

The night of that wake had opened an avenue into a Hawaiian Homestead neighborhood. I could have (and should have) discipled this family to amplify the gospel in an *oikos* of people who would never darken our doorstep. Hale's family could have led a microchurch in that community while remaining active in our congregation. We win some and lose others. The importance is to learn from our losses.

Unfortunately, those who enjoy Church life for any length of time find their relationships focused on the Church, its activities, and quite often its campus. Reinforcing the value of the *oikos* outside the Church is essential if we will equip everyday missionaries, pointing them toward the fields white unto harvest. Identification with an individual or a new group of people precedes influence, and friendmaking should lead to disciplemaking.

A man named Paul is one of my early disciples. We live many miles apart but keep in touch. He recently gathered some friends he met in a coffee shop on a Saturday morning. They decided to meet weekly and have done so for a couple of years. Over time, the atheist began declaring himself an agnostic. A Jewish man now sees Jesus as the Messiah. Paul built a community among those he intended to reach.

Another friend, Danny, is a hip-hop disk jockey. He leads Zoom groups among his peers. A third friend, Jate Earhart, is a computer gamer who began sharing bits and pieces about faith. Those gospel droplets turned into prayer opportunities. He now operates an online "gamers church" numbering more than a thousand participants on several continents.

Each of these three men ministers in a tribal group outside of his home church. As pastors, we should see opportunities that take our people into other tribes, even if the majority of their effort *never* adds to the number of people gracing our chairs on a Sunday.

CHAPTER 22

ROADBLOCKS TO EVERYDAY MISSIONS

We live in dark days, but dark times often precede spiritual awakenings. If you've read this far, you can probably think past *adding* to your attendance while considering the possibilities of *multiplying* your church.

I know a little about spiritual awakenings, having lived through two of them. The first was the Jesus People Movement in the late 1960s and 1970s. We were fortunate to plant the first Hope Chapel during those heady days. The second occurred in Hawaii from the early 1980s until the early 2000s, when we lived at the epicenter.

Thirty people, including children, from our Southern California congregation moved to Oahu in 1983 to plant a church in the small town of Kaneohe. We felt God led us there as a landing platform bent on reaching into Honolulu and the entire state. You might compare this to landing troops in Normandy on the move to Berlin during the Second World War. We began in a small community, where ministry was easier to quantify and manage. From there, we modified our tools and approach to sustain a broader outreach.

At least four times, God visited those islands with spiritual awakenings. The first one, led by Hiram Bingham and Titus Coan between

1820 and 1830, was a precursor of the Second Great Awakening in the United States: the establishment of the Roman Catholic mission in 1840. Both of these early movements multiplied by planting churches. Both were involved in disciplemaking fitted to the culture they met upon arrival; this was E3 evangelism.

In the years following WWII, the Southern Baptists in Hawaii reduced the overall shrinkage by building a church-planting movement. Their approach was often event-centered E2 evangelism. The movement slowed in the late 1970s, even as the Jesus People Movement sparked the birth of a few new congregations. The early 1980s saw stasis in the aftermath of the Jesus People Movement. My friends and I arrived in 1983 with a vision to plant, or help others plant, enough churches to include 1% of the population. Adding 1% to the 4% of self-identified Christians would increase the Christian church by 25%. In other words, 40,000 believers would become 50,000 in a decade.

It took 11 years to reach the goal, which came through many people's energies. We discipled members into missionaries. Some became church planters who did the same. The real power arose when people outside our movement decided that if we could do this, they could too. Collaboration and spiritual unity were significant contributors to success. By 2006, 4% had grown to 73% of self-identifying believers, according to a survey by the Barna organization.[7] And 34% stated they had attended a Protestant or Catholic church meeting within the seven days preceding the study.[8]

It all sounds nice when you look in the rearview mirror, but living through a spiritual awakening is complicated. In both of my "awakening experiences," we faced roadblocks and difficulties that I'll try to explain here.

External Roadblocks

Obstacles to spiritual transformation range from legal impediments to biased people who intentionally obstruct the progress of the Church.

Government and Law

We parachuted into both major church plants, as many planters do. The isolation of only having friends on weekends weighs heavily on those who plant alone or with a tiny core group. A sense that the laws and the government are against them add a heavy burden.

In Manhattan/Hermosa Beach, we quickly outgrew our small parking lot, spilling into the nearby streets. This drew the neighbors' ire and warnings from City Hall. Attempts to distribute literature in public places got stifled, though the Krishnas continued unabated. The Parks Department blocked us from holding services in a community center (though another church used another one in the same city). When we remodeled a bowling alley for church use, a building inspector gave us so much grief that the city fired him over his misdeeds.

Arriving in Hawaii, we immediately tangled with the state over land use and public schools. By law, schools were off-limits to churches (although a few churches occupied them with no difficulty). Honolulu enacted a law against home Bible studies and prayer meetings two years before we arrived. The courts eventually ruled against the city. In the meantime, several churches experienced police intervention. Neighbors harassed our family for legally parking a shipping container on the street in front of our house for three days while we unloaded it. The policeman they hailed was friendly but warned us that the next officer they called might not be.

Our school principal wasn't happy when laws changed allowing churches to rent public schools. A professed Christian, he vowed to "do everything in my power to have you removed because I believe your presence violates the separation of church and state." Three young attorneys in our congregation vowed to sue him, the school board, and the state—soon afterward, he took early retirement.

Pharisees

In Manhattan/Hermosa Beach, we upset churches because we served coffee after service. The coffee resulted from a man challenging us to provide coffee to induce after-service conversations. Local pastors hearing about this called us "the bake sale church," though we didn't even serve cookies, and the coffee was free (serving coffee after Sunday morning church was an anomaly in a time when men wore suits and women wouldn't dare to show up in pants).

In the early days, our congregation was mainly hippies and surfers. Other churches labeled us "Hippity-Hoppity Hope." One pastor attacked the pastor of our first daughter church over his lack of seminary education. His reply to the well-schooled clergyman included comparing the number of people attending our churches to his small following.

Just before we migrated to the state, a pastor in Hawaii wrote a letter advising us to stay home because the state "doesn't need more of your kind of Christians." Middle-class believers regularly criticized rock music in our worship songs. Similar to the man attacking the leader of our first church plant, other pastors attacked us for discipling leaders instead of processing them institutionally.

Many of the things I've described are common to church planters. Some things like coffee or training pastors in a local church are now accepted practices. External factors opposing spiritual transformation will never cease as long as Satan opposes the work of God.

Internal Roadblocks

While examining spiritual roadblocks, we must consider that our enemy sometimes works inside the Church. Sometimes our members can be their own worst enemies regarding everyday missions. At other times we leaders build unintended barriers.

I'm Not an Evangelist

Our people will often express, "I'm not an evangelist" or "Evangelism is for extroverts; I'm an introvert."

These people are not alone. Their declaration includes me, but it doesn't free me from the calling to "do the work of an evangelist." I envy people who lead total strangers to Christ during long airplane flights. Getting on airplanes, I never speak to the stranger sitting next to me. I have difficulty sharing the Lord with my neighbors unless I know them well. I do very well in front of crowds but seldom know what to say to a new acquaintance.

One neighbor barely acknowledges me whenever I greet him. His wife and mine are good friends, but he won't engage. In a recent effort to build community, Ruby and I shared an overflow of our tomato garden with our neighbors. I knocked on two doors with great success but held back from this man's home. My wife delivered the tomatoes. I was appalled when she informed him that she delivered the fruit while I sat in the car because "my husband is too shy to come to the door." The good news is that her statement brought a smile to his face. I came off as a wimp, but at least we got a smile from our reserved neighbor.

My life is replete with stories like this one. As a pastor, I would include them in my teachings. When equipping members as everyday missionaries, sharing my fear stories helped Church members get past their own. Evangelism for Christ-followers is an obedience issue rather than an option.

Fear of Rejection

People often reject a messenger along with a message they dislike. Many people fear that if they speak of spiritual things, they and their words might damage a friendship. This problem compounded when speaking of religion in the workplace somehow got confused with the separation of church and state. Our members are often unsure of boundaries when sharing spiritual realities.

Moses comes to mind. He knew his weakness as a communicator and also feared that his people would reject him. It is important to remember that God supported him through his brother, Aaron. I try to help people make disciples among non-believers with a partner whenever possible. The individual may be a boyfriend, girlfriend, spouse, or workmate. Perhaps Jesus commissioned his disciples to work in pairs because some were as introverted as my friends and me.

Sharing faith requires faith, especially when a person believes doing so might cost them a friendship. As equippers, we need to acknowledge this. Again, this is a matter of obedience. We must overcome the sense that life is about us and present our bodies as a living sacrifice, which is true worship. In truth, the gospel may cost someone a friendship, but it cost the apostles their lives. Finally, I remind others that they are only responsible for faithfulness. The fruitfulness belongs to God.

THE POWER OF REACHABLE GOALS

Our zeal for the Great Commission can create roadblocks to accomplishing it. Jesus' command to make disciples is the Church's mission, but if you over-emphasize the *assignment*, you may fall into a legalistic trap. Overstate personal *vision,* and you will unhinge your people from the mission by focusing on growing numbers rather than making disciples.

Mission-Driven Guilt

I'm at an age where weight loss is ever more challenging. I used to be able to shed pounds by increasing exercise or reducing my intake of calories. Those options still work, just not as well. There is another problem. Whenever I violate the diet for a couple of days, I feel down on myself and eat more to compensate for my negative feelings. On the other side of this equation, a couple of good days motivate me to discipline myself better.

Sometimes our members lack inner encouragement to share their faith because they failed at it before. Often they receive our teachings about the mission as proof of their inadequacy. People who feel inadequate cannot meet the challenge we offer. Negative feelings generate more negative feelings.

The antidote to this is to offer encouragement, to lead with a vision of what *could* be rather than press the mission of what *should* be. You do this primarily by telling stories. Stories from the congregation build courage in other members. By introducing heromaking into the narrative, you invite others to share the action. Real-life stories present a bite-sized vision, making the work of an everyday missionary doable. Constantly thumping the mission cannot top an image of the mission as it blossoms in the lives of ordinary people.

Dreaming Too Big

The adage "What gets measured is what gets done" can work for you, or it can work against you. Measuring attendance can result in counting chairs filled rather than disciples made. Conversely, tallying disciples made can get out of hand if your goals are unrealistic.

Jeff is planting a new church after 39 years of leading a congregation from which he launched several others. He and his wife parachuted into a new city, where they both enjoy the rejuvenation born by new projects. He told me that his wife was busy plotting how all 350,000 people would come to Christ through their efforts. Jeff stopped the roller coaster by asking her, "How many could come to Christ in the next decade in churches we plant and those they plant?" His question helped reduce the goal to something manageable.

Before we planted the first Hope Chapel, a mentor asked me to identify how many people lived within a 10-mile radius of our tiny building. He then asked me to extrapolate how many of those would be in our colossal church (wishful thinking) in 10 years. That circle included a significant business center and a massive cluster of industrial buildings where no one lived. Some neighborhoods were so racially and culturally dissimilar that we would never adequately reach them until one of their number joined us, bringing the capacity to reach back into their own community.

For us, the hardest-to-reach people lived in the second-largest concentration of wealth in L.A. County. The circle did include a significant number of people who fit our socioeconomic profile. However, the circle was too large, and it didn't account for the many people in it who would never identify with us.

A better circle to describe as a congregation's Jerusalem would be smaller—perhaps a three- or five-mile radius. That way, it wouldn't discourage leaders or members. A reasonable percentage of the population to disciple would allow leaders to measure and celebrate progress toward their goals. A local congregation's Judea is the next natural radius beyond its particular Jerusalem.

Any scorecard should include the number of churches planted. Ruby and I recently joined a church that has produced 13 others across the globe in its 15 years of existence. They just celebrated one church plant reproducing itself, sowing the seed of a multiplication movement. They now intend to plant microchurches while investing in larger congregations. Their problem is that while reproducing far from home they haven't yet cracked the code for San Diego County or the rest of California. Their Jerusalem is the city of San Diego, and they are connecting to the ends of the earth. Everyday missionaries making disciples everywhere are the solution to their dilemma.

You may never have planted a church, and doing so may seem too large an undertaking. This being the case, I suggest you look at your disciplemaking continuum for meaningful goals. Ask yourself these questions: How many groups do you have? How many leaders have apprentices? How many have more than one apprentice? How many people attend these in-house microchurches? How many of your members are actively discipling another person? How many people would qualify as microchurch missionaries if you lowered the threshold for the mission?

The answers to these questions will help you permeate your surrounding culture with the gospel in small but significant ways. They can display immediate progress toward realistic and reachable goals, encouraging and inspiring your members to stay on mission.

CHAPTER 24

LEADING AS A MISSIONARY OVERSEER

Your church and mine rise and fall on leadership—*our* leadership. How you perceive yourself influences the outcome of your ministry. Equipping others is a given, but qualifying them sometimes gets us into trouble.

Ecclesiology

Each congregation has its particular polity or way of doing things. I call these the house rules. We often disguise our rules as theology. Local and denominational theology or ecclesiology can impede disciplemaking, evangelism, and church multiplication.

Putting Jesus first in our thinking will change how we structure our ministries. Put the church and its rules first, and you generate problems. The simplicity of justification by faith qualifies everyday missionaries; artificial thresholds, like classes attended or not, can disqualify them.

My friend, Brian Sanders, helped me clarify this in his book *Microchurch: A Smaller Way*.[9] I'll describe my interpretation here, but you should look at his book for more on the subject.

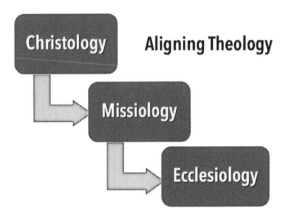

Suppose you begin with Christology, or your understanding of Jesus and his mission. Then you move to missiology, which is your understanding and experience in the ministry outlined in the Great Commission. Christology comingled with missional practice should birth a working ecclesiology or body of church polity. Keep these in the correct order, and your ministry will thrive, grow, and multiply. Confuse them, and you'll fall short of your potential.

Shepherd vs. Equipper

Limit yourself to shepherding the sheep, and they remain sheep while you stay busy tending to needs and hurts. Reposition yourself as an equipper, and your members will look after those needs and hurts while exploring their identities as God's unique masterpieces. Understanding identity leads to exploring giftedness and calling. As an equipper, you move from the small circle of a single congregation to leading a movement. Even a megachurch is smaller than a movement.

Pastor vs. Overseer

Speaking of movements, let's investigate the use of the term *overseer* in the life of James in Acts 15. The terms *pastor, elder,* and *overseer* overlap in meaning; however, let's focus on this particular word as it would apply to this man. His evolution carries substantial implications for us today.

Before the Jerusalem Council, the New Testament identifies James, the half-brother of Jesus, as a doubter, then later as the overseer of the churches in Judea. The decisions rendered him what you might call a "missionary overseer" responsible for the ministry to the myriad ethnicities and geography of what the Bible calls Gentiles. In this role, he assumed responsibility for the future of the Church. His duty and behavior implied the eventual evangelization of the ends of the earth—including Hawaii, the islands further removed from landmass than any other.

At the close of the Jerusalem Council, when welcoming Gentiles into the Church, James graduated from a single-location leader to one overseeing the future of the gospel as it would travel places he would never venture. His ministry would only reach fruition through the efforts of other people.

Missionary Overseer

So, I want to leave you with this challenge: can you reposition yourself as a missionary overseer? You must equip and free others to accomplish all God puts in your jurisdiction to achieve full outreach potential.

Let's close with three statements from Ecclesiastes:

- If you wait for perfect conditions, you will never get anything done (Ecclesiastes 11:4, TLB).
- Keep on sowing your seed, for you never know which will grow—perhaps it all will (Ecclesiastes 11:6, TLB).

- For the preacher was not only a wise man but a good teacher; he not only taught what he knew to the people, but he taught them in an interesting manner (Ecclesiastes 12:10, TLB).

The fields are white. The task is straightforward. It is up to us to equip our members to evangelize in a dark and even hostile world. It is still required of a steward that a person be found faithful. Go for it!

ENDNOTES

1. APEST is an acronym for apostles, prophets, evangelists, shepherds, and teachers from Ephesians 4:11.

2. George Barna, *We Have Seen the Future: The Demise of Christianity in Los Angeles County* (The Barna Research Group, 1990).

3. For more on Troy Evans see https://www.rapidgrowthmedia.com.

4. Follow the "About" link for more: https://www.thisismission.org/about-1.

5. Matthew Rose, "The Liberalism of Richard John Neuhaus," *National Affairs*, Summer 2022.

6. Dave Ferguson and Warren Bird, *Heromaker: The Five Essential Practices for Leaders to Multiply Leaders* (Grand Rapids: Zondervan, 2018).

7. The Barna Group, *The State of Faith in Hawaii* (Ventura: Barna Resources, 2011), 73.

8. Ibid., 31.

9. Brian Sanders, *Microchurches: A Smaller Way* (Grand Rapids: Zondervan, 2019).

ABOUT THE AUTHOR

Ralph Moore is the founding pastor of three churches that grew into the Hope Chapel movement, now numbering more than 2,300 churches worldwide. These are the offspring of the 70+ congregations launched from Ralph's hands-on disciplemaking efforts.

He currently serves as "church multiplication catalyzer" for Exponential. In addition to this, he travels the globe, teaching church multiplication to pastors in startup movements. He has authored several books, including *Making Disciples*, *How to Multiply Your Church*, *Starting a New Church*, *Defeating Anxiety*, and *Let Go of the Ring: The Hope Chapel Story*. Check out his blog at www.RalphMoore.net.

Made in the USA
Las Vegas, NV
20 December 2022

63752302R00077